Presented to _____

by _____

on _____

Text © 2004 The Livingstone Corporation. © 2004 Standard Publishing, Cincinnati, Ohio. A division of Standex International Corporation. All rights reserved. Sprout logo is a trademark of Standard Publishing. Printed in China. Project editor: Lindsay Black. Design: Robert Glover. Typesetting: SettingPace.

Produced with the assistance of The Livingstone Corporation (www.LivingstoneCorporation.com). Project authors: Emily Malone and Jeanette Dall. Project consultant: Dr. Mary Manz Simon. Project staff: Betsy Todt Schmitt, Dr. Bruce B. Barton, David R. Veerman, and Mary Horner Collins.

10 09 08 07 06 05 04   9 8 7 6 5 4 3 2 1

ISBN 0-7847-1599-8

One Way Bible

illustrated by Joe Van Severen

Standard Publishing

cincinnati, ohio

Table of Contents

Old Testament

New Testament

God's Special Creation

What makes you special? Maybe you're good at art, or you can run fast. Maybe you're good at making friends. Whatever is unique about you, God made you that way. Find out more about his special creation...

In the beginning God created the heavens and the earth. God said, "Let there be light," and there was light. Then he separated the light from the darkness and called them "day" and "night." Together these made up one day.

Then God said, "Let there be space between the waters." And God called the space "sky."

And God said, "Let the waters below the sky be gathered into one place so dry ground may appear." Then God said, "Let the land burst with every sort of plant, and let there be trees that grow fruit."

And God said, "Let bright lights appear in the sky to separate the day from the night. They will mark the seasons, days, and years." So God made the sun, moon, and stars to shine down upon the earth.

And God said, "Let the waters swarm with fish and other life, and let the skies be filled with birds."

And God said, "Let the earth be filled with every kind of animal." God made all sorts of wild animals, farm animals, and small animals.

Then God said, "Let us make people in our image, to be like ourselves. They will be masters over all life."

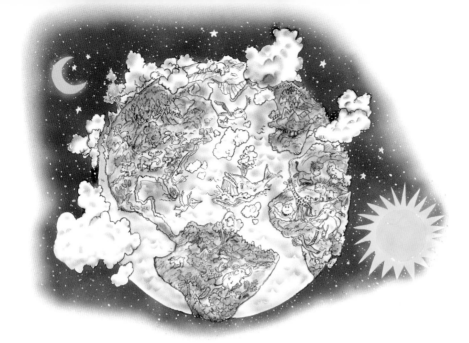

God blessed them and told them, "Have children and fill the earth and be in charge of it." Then God looked at all he had made and saw that it was excellent.

So the creation of the heavens and the earth was completed in six days. And God blessed the seventh day and called it holy, because it was the day when he rested from his work of creation.

Story based on Genesis 1:1-2:3 as it appears in the New Living Translation®.

Let's talk about it...

Everything God made was good—and God made you. He knew just what he was doing when he gave you your hair and eyes and skin and brain. There is no other person exactly like you on this earth. Isn't that amazing? You are amazing. You are God's special creation.

You made us . . . and you crowned us with glory and honor.
Psalm 8:5, NLT

We're in Big Trouble!

When someone gives you instructions, do you obey? What happens if you don't? The first man and woman ever created decided to disobey God.
Examine the consequences...

The LORD placed the man in the Garden of Eden to care for it. But God warned him: "You may eat any fruit except fruit from the tree of knowledge. If you eat this fruit, you will surely die."

And the LORD said, "It is not good for the man to be alone." So God made a woman and took her to Adam.

Now the serpent, the most clever of all creatures, asked the woman, "Did God really say you must not eat the fruit in the garden?"

"Of course we may eat it," the woman said. "But if we eat or touch the fruit from the tree at the center of the garden, we will die."

"You won't die!" the serpent said with a hiss. "God knows that you will become just like him if you eat it."

So she ate some of the fruit and also gave some to Adam. Then they understood what they had done. They felt shame at being naked.

They heard the LORD walking in the garden, so they hid. The LORD called, "Where are you?" Adam answered, "I was afraid because I was naked."

"Who told you that you were naked?" God asked. "Have you eaten the fruit I commanded you not to?"

"Yes," Adam admitted, "but the woman you gave me brought me the fruit." When God asked the woman why she did it, she said, "The serpent tricked me."

So the LORD said to the serpent, "You'll be punished and will crawl in the dust as long as you live." Then God told Adam and Eve they would be punished too. He said, "You will have pain, and you will have to work hard."

Then God made them leave the Garden of Eden forever.

Story based on Genesis 2:15–3:24 as it appears in the New Living Translation®.

Let's talk about it...

Rules are hard to follow sometimes, aren't they? Adam and Eve found that out when they disobeyed the only rule that God gave them. God gave them that rule because he loved them and knew what would happen if they disobeyed. God gives us rules for the same reasons. He loves us and wants to keep us safe!

You will be blessed if you obey the commands of the LORD, your God.

Deuteronomy 11:27, NLT

Safe from the Storm

Have you ever been afraid during a bad storm? Where did you find safety? Who took care of you? This story is about a huge and very dangerous storm. But look at how God protected his people...

The LORD saw the people's wickedness. He knew that their thoughts were totally evil. And the LORD said, "I will completely wipe out all these people that I have created. Yes, and I will destroy all the animals and birds, too. I am sorry I ever made them." But Noah pleased the LORD because he obeyed.

So God said to Noah, "Make a boat from wood and seal it with tar. Make it 450 feet long, 75 feet wide, and 45 feet high.

"I am about to cover the earth with a flood that will destroy every living thing. But I promise to keep you and your family safe in the boat. Bring a pair of every kind of animal with you to keep them alive."

So Noah did everything exactly as God commanded.

When Noah was 600 years old, the underground waters burst out of the earth, and the rain fell for forty days. All the living things on Earth died.

But God remembered Noah and all the animals in the boat. So the flood gradually went down, and the boat came to rest on the mountains of Ararat.

After forty more days, Noah sent out a raven that flew back and forth until the earth was dry. Then he kept sending out a dove until it didn't return.

Then God said to Noah, "Leave the boat, all of you. I am making an agreement with you and your descendants. I promise never to send another flood to kill all living creatures and destroy the earth. I am giving you something to show that I will always remember my promise to you and all living creatures. I have placed my rainbow in the clouds. It is the sign of my permanent promise to you and to all the earth."

Story based on Genesis 6:5–8:19; 9:8–13 as it appears in the New Living Translation®.

Let's talk about it...

What a terrible storm! Can you imagine that much rain? But, just as God promised, he kept Noah and his family safe. God promises to take care of us, too. So the next time you are afraid—whether it's during a storm or any other time—remember God's promise to protect and keep you safe.

I will lie down in peace and sleep, for you alone,
O LORD, will keep me safe.
Psalm 4:8, NLT

Look at Our Tower!

Show-offs think they are really good at something—and want everyone to know it. Maybe you know someone who lets everyone know that he is the best. In this story people wanted to show off their skills.
Discover what God thinks about show-offs...

At one time the whole world spoke one language and used the same words. As the people traveled east, they decided to live in the land of Babylonia. Once they were settled, they began to talk about building projects.

"Come," they said, "let's make great piles of bricks. Then we can use them to build a great city with a tower that reaches to the skies to show how great we are! This will bring us together and keep us from scattering all over the world."

But the LORD came down to see the city and the tower the people were building.

"Look!" he said. "They are able to do this because they all speak the same language and have one government. Just think of what worse things they will do later. Nothing will be impossible for them! Come, let's go down and give them different languages to speak. Then they won't be able to understand each other."

In that way, the LORD scattered them all over the earth; and that ended the building of the city. The city was called Babel, because it was there that the LORD

confused the people. He gave them many languages
and caused them to scatter across the earth.

Story based on Genesis 11:1-9 as it appears in the New Living Translation®.

Let's talk about it...

These people wanted to show everyone that they could
build a really tall tower. But God made sure the people
knew that they couldn't do anything without him. If you
are good at something—getting good grades, singing
beautifully, or playing a sport—do it really well. Thank
God for what he has made you able to do.

For all the earth is the LORD's,
and he has set the world in order.

1 Samuel 2:8, NLT

A Big Change for Abram

Changes can be scary. It's hard to do something you have never done before. In this story God told Abram to make a big change in his life.

Read about what happened to Abram...

Then the LORD told Abram, "Leave your country, your relatives, and your father's house, and go to the land that I will show you. I will cause you to become the father of a great nation. I will bless you and make you famous, and I will make you a blessing to others. I will bless those who bless you and curse those who curse you. All the families of the earth will be blessed through you."

So Abram left as the LORD had told him, and Lot went with him. Abram was seventy-five years old when he left Haran. He took his wife Sarai, his nephew Lot, and all his wealth—his animals and all the people who had joined his household at Haran— and finally arrived in Canaan. Traveling through Canaan, they came to a place near Shechem and set up camp beside the oak at Moreh. At that time, the Canaanites lived in the area.

Then the LORD appeared to Abram and said, "I am going to give this land to your children and grandchildren." And Abram built an altar there to remember the LORD's visit. After that, Abram traveled southward and set up camp in the hill country between Bethel on the west and Ai on the east. He built an altar

there and worshiped the LORD. Then Abram began to travel south toward the desert of the Negev.

Story based on Genesis 12:1-9 as it appears in the New Living Translation®.

Let's talk about it...

It must have been hard for Abram to leave his home and everyone he knew, but Abram trusted in God. And God took care of Abram in the new place. God might tell you to do something different and scary. But you can trust that he'll be with you. Whenever you face a big change—a new class, a new neighborhood—God is with you and will take care of you.

I will walk among you; I will be your God, and you will be my people.
Leviticus 26:12, NLT

Too Many to Count

Next time you're outside at night, look up and count the stars. You'll probably get called inside before you can finish. In this story God promised to bless Abram with more descendants than he could ever count.
Let's see what happened...

The LORD spoke to Abram in a vision and said, "Do not be afraid, Abram. I will protect you, and your reward will be great."

But Abram said, "O LORD, what good are all your blessings when I don't even have a son? You have given me no children, so one of my servants will have to be my heir."

Then the LORD said to him, "No, your servant will not be your heir. You will have a son of your own to inherit everything I am giving you." Then the LORD brought Abram outside beneath the night sky. God told him, "Look up into the heavens and count the stars if you can. Your descendants will be like that— too many to count!" And Abram believed the LORD, and the LORD said Abram's faith was right.

When Abram was ninety-nine years old, the LORD appeared and said, "I am God Almighty; serve me faithfully and live right. I will make an agreement with you to make you into a mighty nation." At this, Abram fell facedown in the dust. Then God said to him, "This is my agreement with you: I will make you the father of many nations! What's more, I am changing your

name. Now you will be called Abraham, for you will be the father of many nations. I will give you millions of descendants who will become many new nations.

"This agreement will continue between me and your family forever. Yes, I will give all this land of Canaan to you and to your descendants forever. And I will be their God."

Story based on Genesis 15:1-6; 17:1-8 as it appears in the New Living Translation®.

Let's talk about it...

Abraham was feeling bad because he didn't have even one son. But God promised to give him more descendants than there are stars in the sky. Wow! God is like that—he gives us so much more than we could ever imagine. We need to be like Abraham and believe that God will keep his promises.

Your words are truth, and you have promised these good things to me.

2 Samuel 7:28, NLT

Abraham's Big Test

You probably have taken all kinds of tests—multiple choice tests, spelling tests, fitness tests. But have you ever taken a God-test? In this story God gave Abraham a really, really big test on obedience.

Find out what God asked Abraham to do...

God tested Abraham's faith and obedience. "Abraham!" God called. "Take your only son, Isaac, and go to the land of Moriah. Sacrifice him there as an offering."

The next morning Abraham saddled his donkey and took two of his servants with him, along with his son Isaac. Then he set out for the land of Moriah. When Abraham saw the place in the distance, he told the servants, "Stay here with the donkey. Isaac and I will travel a little farther and worship. Then we'll come back."

Abraham placed the wood for the burnt offering on Isaac's shoulders. He himself carried the knife and the fire. As the two of them went on together, Isaac asked, "Where is the lamb for the sacrifice?"

"God will give us a lamb," Abraham answered.

When they arrived at the place where God had told Abraham to go, he built an altar. Then he tied Isaac up, and placed him on the altar over the wood. Then Abraham lifted the knife to kill his son as a sacrifice to the LORD. At that moment the angel of the LORD shouted, "Abraham! Abraham! Lay down the knife. Do not hurt the boy in any way. Now I know that you truly

obey God. You have not kept back even your beloved son from me."

Then Abraham looked up and saw a ram caught in a bush. So he sacrificed it as a burnt offering instead of his son. He named the place "The LORD Will Provide."

Then the angel of the LORD called out, "The LORD says: Because you have obeyed me, I promise that I will bless you richly. I will multiply your descendants like the sand on the seashore. All the nations of the earth will be blessed because you have obeyed me."

Story based on Genesis 22:1-18 as it appears in the New Living Translation®.

Let's talk about it...

God wanted to see if Abraham would obey him—and Abraham passed the test. Abraham loved God so much that he would do anything God asked. Not many of us will have a *big* test on obedience like Abraham's. But God calls us to obey him every day, by doing things like sharing with others and telling the truth. Are you passing the test?

If you love me, obey my commandments.
John 14:15, NLT

What's It Worth to You?

Think of the most valuable item you own. Would you trade it for a cookie or a bag of chips? Probably not. In this story Esau had something very valuable. Inspect what he ended up trading it for...

When Isaac was forty years old, he married Rebekah. Isaac begged the LORD to give Rebekah a child. So the LORD answered Isaac's prayer. Rebekah would have twins. But the two children struggled with each other inside her. So she went to the LORD and asked "Why is this happening?"

And the LORD told her, "The sons inside you will become two enemy nations. One nation will be stronger than the other; the descendants of your older son will serve the descendants of your younger son."

When the twins were born, the first son was very red. They called him Esau because he was covered with so much hair. The other twin was born holding onto Esau's heel. So they called him Jacob.

Esau became a skillful hunter who loved the outdoors, while Jacob liked to stay at home. Isaac loved Esau because he brought home the meat Isaac liked, but Rebekah favored Jacob.

One day when Jacob was cooking stew, Esau arrived home tired and hungry from a hunt. Esau said to Jacob, "I'm starved! Give me some of your red stew."

Jacob answered, "All right, but trade me your birthright for it." (A birthright was a special honor given to the firstborn son.)

"I'm dying of starvation!" said Esau. "What good is my birthright to me now?"

But Jacob insisted, "Promise me right now that it is mine." So Esau promised and sold all his rights as firstborn to Jacob. Then Esau ate and went about his business. He did not care that he sold his birthright.

Story based on Genesis 25:19-34 as it appears in the New Living Translation®.

Let's talk about it...

Imagine trading your special privileges as the firstborn for a *bowl of stew*. What was Esau thinking? Sometimes, though, we are like Esau. We forget what's really important, like when we watch TV or play on the computer rather than being with friends or reading our Bible. Esau's story helps us remember to treasure what is most valuable—our special friendship with God.

Store your treasures in heaven,
where they will never become moth-eaten or rusty.
Matthew 6:20, NLT

Getting to Know God

How do you get to know someone? Maybe you spend time with that person, talking on the phone or doing stuff together. In this story Jacob got to know about God in a very interesting way.

Let's see what happened...

Jacob left Beersheba and traveled toward Haran. At sundown he arrived at a good place to set up camp and stopped there for the night. Jacob found a stone for a pillow and lay down to sleep. As he slept, he dreamed of a stairway that reached from Earth to Heaven. He saw the angels of God going up and down on it.

At the top of the stairway stood the LORD, and he said, "I am the LORD, the God of your grandfather, Abraham, and the God of your father, Isaac. The ground you are lying on belongs to you. I will give it to you and your descendants. Your descendants will cover the land from east to west and from north to south. All the families of the earth will be blessed through you and your descendants. What's more, I will be with you, and I will protect you wherever you go. I will someday bring you safely back to this land. I will be with you all the time until you have everything I have promised."

Then Jacob woke up and said, "Surely the LORD is in this place." He was afraid and said, "What an awesome place this is! It is none other than the house of God—the gateway to Heaven!" The next morning he got up very early. He took the stone he had used as a pillow and set it upright as a memorial of his dream.

22

Then Jacob made this promise: "If God will be with me and protect me on this journey, and if he will bring me back safely to my father, then I will make the LORD my God. This stone will be a place for worshiping God. I will give God a tenth of everything he gives me."

Story based on Genesis 28:10-22 as it appears in the New Living Translation®.

Let's talk about it...

God used a dream to tell Jacob who he was and what he would do for Jacob. God may not give you a dream, but he does want you to know him. So how can you get to know God? You can hear about God at church. You can learn about him as you read the Bible and pray. God knows and loves you. He wants you to know and love him, too.

Happy are those who are strong in the LORD.
Psalm 84:5, NLT

The Trouble with Jealousy

How do you feel when your friend gets the really cool bike that you want? Or when the class "brain" gets straight A's—again? It's easy to feel angry, even jealous. But jealousy can cause big problems.

Check it out in Joseph's story...

Joseph, Jacob's son, often watched his father's flocks with his brothers. But Joseph told his father the bad things his brothers were doing. Now Jacob loved Joseph more than any of his other children. So one day he gave Joseph a beautiful robe. But his brothers hated Joseph because their father liked him the best.

One night Joseph had a dream and told it to his brothers. This caused them to hate him even more. Then Joseph had another dream and told his father and brothers about it. But while his brothers were jealous of Joseph, his father gave it some thought and wondered what it all meant.

Soon after this, Joseph's brothers took their father's flocks to Shechem. Jacob said to Joseph, "Go and see how your brothers and the flocks are getting along."

When Joseph's brothers saw him coming in the distance, they made plans to kill him. But Reuben came to Joseph's rescue. "Let's just throw him alive into this pit here." So when Joseph arrived, they pulled off his beautiful robe and threw him into the pit. Then they noticed that traders on camels were coming toward them.

24

So when the traders came by, his brothers pulled Joseph out of the pit and sold him for twenty pieces of silver. The Ishmaelite traders took him to Egypt.

Then Joseph's brothers killed a goat, dipped the robe in its blood, and took it to their father. Jacob recognized it at once. "Yes," he said, "it is my son's robe. A wild animal has attacked and eaten him." Jacob cried and was sad about his son for many days.

Story based on Genesis 37:2-34 as it appears in the New Living Translation®.

Let's talk about it...

Joseph's brothers did some terrible things out of jealousy. We all have jealous feelings at times. Maybe someone is a better reader than you or a friend makes the team when you don't. But jealousy doesn't make us feel better, and it can make us do unfair things. When jealous feelings bubble up, we need to ask for God's help *before* trouble happens.

Love is not jealous or boastful or proud.

I Corinthians 13:4, NLT

Forgive and Forget!

What do you do when someone teases you or hurts you? Do you forgive that person, or do you try to get even? Joseph had that choice when his brothers, who had sold him into slavery, showed up in Egypt. *Discover Joseph's decision...*

No food was growing in Canaan. Twice Joseph's brothers went to Egypt asking for food. They asked Joseph, but they did not recognize Joseph. On the second trip, Joseph insisted they bring Benjamin, the youngest brother, or they would not receive any food. The brothers did, but Joseph still wanted to test them. So he had a guard put his silver cup in Benjamin's sack. Now the brothers stood before Joseph. He accused Benjamin of stealing Joseph's silver cup.

Judah said, "Oh, my lord, what can we say to you? How can we prove our innocence? God is punishing us for our sins. My lord, we returned to be your slaves."

"No," Joseph said. "Only the man who stole the cup will be my slave. The rest of you may go home."

Then Judah stepped forward and asked to take Benjamin's place. Judah explained to Joseph that it might kill his father if Benjamin did not return.

Joseph could stand it no longer. "I am Joseph! Is my father still alive?" But his brothers were too shocked to speak! "These two years without food will grow to seven. God has sent me here ahead of you to keep your families alive so that you will become a great nation.

"Tell my father: God has made me master of Egypt. Come to me right away! I will take care of you, for there are still five years without food ahead of us."

Crying with joy, Joseph hugged Benjamin, and Benjamin also began to cry. Then Joseph kissed each of his brothers and cried over them. Then they began talking freely with him.

Story based on Genesis 43:1–44:34; 45:1-15 as it appears in the New Living Translation®.

Let's talk about it...

Joseph's brothers treated him very badly. But instead of getting even, Joseph forgave them. Amazing, right? Guess what? We can have that same forgiveness. When we lie, disobey our parents, or hurt a friend, God will forgive us. He doesn't treat us as we deserve. As we understand God's forgiveness, we can be like Joseph and forgive those who hurt us.

Remember, the Lord forgave you,
so you must forgive others.
Colossians 3:13, NLT

Who's in Control?

All it takes is a flick of a switch to move a remote-control car. With the controls in hand, you can make the car do anything you want. Pharaoh, the ruler of Egypt, thought he could do anything he wanted. Decide who was really in control of Egypt...

A new king came to the throne of Egypt who knew nothing about Joseph or the good things he had done. The king was worried because there were so many Israelites. So the Egyptians made the Israelites their slaves, hoping to wear them down under heavy burdens. But the more the Egyptians treated them badly, the more children God gave the Israelites!

Then Pharaoh gave this order: "Throw all the newborn Israelite boys into the Nile River."

During this time, a certain Israelite woman had a son. She kept him hidden for three months. But when she could no longer hide him, she put the baby in a waterproof basket and laid it in the Nile River. The baby's sister then stood at a distance, watching to see what would happen to him.

Soon, one of Pharaoh's daughters came to bathe in the river. When the princess saw the little basket among the reeds, she told one of her servant girls to get it. As the princess opened it, she found the baby boy. "He must be one of the Israelite children," she said.

Then the baby's sister asked the princess, "Should I find an Israelite woman to care for the baby?"

"Yes, do!" the princess replied. So the girl rushed home and called the baby's mother.

"Take this child home and care for him for me," the princess told her. "I will pay you for your help." So the baby's mother took her baby home and cared for him.

Later, when he was older, the child's mother brought him back to the princess. She adopted him as her own son. The princess named him Moses, for she said, "I drew him out of the water."

Story based on Exodus 1:8-2:10 as it appears in the New Living Translation®.

Let's talk about it...

Pharaoh thought he could control God's people by killing all the baby boys. But God had another plan. God protected baby Moses, allowed the princess to find the baby, and even allowed Moses' mother to care for him. Sometimes this world is scary. That's when we need to remember who really is in control—God!

LORD, there is no one like you! For you are great, and your name is full of power.
Jeremiah 10:6, NLT

Who, Me?

Sometimes when we are asked to do something that's hard, we think that we can't. That's how Moses felt when God asked him to return to Egypt. But God reminded Moses that he wouldn't be alone.

Let's find out what happens...

One day Moses was watching the sheep in the wilderness near Sinai, the mountain of God. Suddenly, the angel of the LORD appeared to him as a blazing fire in a bush. Moses was amazed because the bush was full of flames, but it didn't burn up.

When the LORD saw that he had caught Moses' attention, God called to him from the bush.

"Here I am!" Moses replied.

"Do not come any closer," God told him. "Take off your sandals, for you are standing on holy ground. I am the God of your ancestors—Abraham, Isaac, and Jacob." When Moses heard this, he hid his face in his hands because he was afraid to look at God.

Then the LORD told him, "I have heard my people's cries for rescue from their harsh slave drivers. Yes, I am aware of their suffering. So I have come to rescue them and lead them out of Egypt into their own good land. Now go, for I am sending you to Pharaoh. You will lead my people out of Egypt."

"But who am I to appear before Pharaoh?" Moses asked God. "How can I lead the Israelites?"

Then God told him, "I will be with you."

But Moses argued, "If I go to the people of Israel and say, 'The God of your ancestors has sent me to you,' they won't believe me."

God replied, "I AM THE ONE WHO ALWAYS IS. Just tell them, 'I AM has sent me to you.'"

Story based on Exodus 3:1-14 as it appears in the New Living Translation®.

Let's talk about it...

Moses wasn't sure he would be able to do what God wanted. But how talented we are isn't what's most important. What is important is how powerful God is. If God tells us to do something, he will help us do it. What has God asked you to do? Forgive a friend? Obey your parents? Share with others? Whatever it is, ask God to help you—he will.

For I can do everything with the help of Christ who gives me the strength I need.

Philippians 4:13, NLT

The Great Escape

Here's the scene. There's a big, mean dog on one side of the street and the school bully on the other. You must walk down the street to get to school. How do you escape trouble?

The Israelites in the story felt like this...

Word reached the king of Egypt that the Israelites were not planning to return to Egypt. So all Pharaoh's soldiers were used to chase them.

As Pharaoh and his army approached, the people of Israel could see them in the distance. The people began to panic, and they cried out to the LORD for help. Then they turned against Moses and complained to him. But Moses told the people, "Don't be afraid. The LORD himself will fight for you."

Then the LORD said to Moses, "Use your shepherd's staff—hold it out over the Red Sea, and a path will open up through the sea."

Then Moses raised his hand over the sea, and the LORD opened up a path through the water with a strong east wind. So the people of Israel walked through the sea on dry ground, with walls of water on each side! Then the Egyptians followed them. But the LORD looked down on the Egyptian army and threw them into confusion.

When all the Israelites were on the other side, the LORD said to Moses, "Raise your hand over the sea again." So Moses raised his hand over the sea. The water

roared back into its usual place. None of the Egyptians who had chased the Israelites into the sea survived.

The people of Israel saw the LORD's mighty power used against the Egyptians. Then they trusted the LORD and put their faith in him and his servant Moses.

Story based on Exodus 14:5-31 as it appears in the New Living Translation®.

Let's talk about it...

Even though the Israelites were stuck between the Red Sea and Pharaoh's army, God provided an unexpected way out. The good news is that God will do that for us, too. Whether it's a science test or a classmate on the playground who is teasing you—God is there. When it feels like there's no way out, God will help you through.

Remember that you were once slaves in Egypt and that the LORD your God brought you out with amazing power and mighty deeds.

Deuteronomy 5:15, NLT

What's Your Complaint?

Does this sound familiar: "When are we going to get there?" "I'm hungry!" "I'm thirsty!" The Israelites were tired and hungry from their journey out of Egypt. But instead of asking God for help, they complained. Look at what happened...

A month after leaving Egypt, the whole community of Israel spoke against Moses and Aaron.

"Oh, that we were back in Egypt," they moaned. "You have brought us into this desert to starve us."

Then the LORD said to Moses, "Look, I'm going to rain down food from Heaven. The people can go out each day and pick up as much food as they need for that day. I will test them in this to see whether they will follow my instructions. Tell them to pick up twice as much as usual on the sixth day of each week."

Then Moses and Aaron called a meeting of all the people of Israel. They said, "The LORD will give you meat to eat in the evening and bread in the morning. He has heard all your complaints against him. Yes, your complaints are against the LORD, not against us."

That evening many quail arrived and covered the camp. The next morning the desert was wet with dew. When the dew disappeared, thin flakes, white like frost, covered the ground.

And Moses told them, "This is the food the LORD has given you. The LORD says that each household should gather as much as it needs. Pick up two quarts for each person."

So the people of Israel went out and gathered this food. Those who gathered a lot had nothing left over, and those who gathered only a little had enough. Each family had just what it needed.

In time, the food became known as manna. It was white and tasted like honey cakes.

Story based on Exodus 16:1-31 as it appears in the New Living Translation®.

Let's talk about it...

How quickly the Israelites forgot all that God had done for them. Yet, in spite of their complaints, God heard them and provided exactly what they needed. Sometimes when things don't go our way, we complain. That's when we need to change our attitude and look to God. He will provide what we need.

All eyes look to you for help;
you give them their food as they need it.
Psalm 145:15, NLT

Following the Crowd

When friends pressure you to do something—even when you know it's wrong—it's hard to ignore them. While Moses is away, the Israelites try to make Aaron do the wrong thing.

Read how Aaron responded...

When Moses failed to come back down the mountain right away, the people went to Aaron. "Look," they said, "make us some gods who can lead us. We don't know what has happened to Moses."

So Aaron told the people to bring him their gold. Then he took the gold, melted it, and molded it into the shape of a calf. The people exclaimed, "O Israel, these are the gods who brought you out of Egypt!"

When Aaron saw how excited the people were about it, he built an altar. He announced, "Tomorrow there will be a festival to the LORD!"

Then the LORD told Moses, "Quick! Go down the mountain! The people you brought from Egypt are sinning. They have already turned from the way I commanded them to live."

Then the LORD said, "I have seen how stubborn these people are. They don't obey me. Now my anger will blaze against them and destroy them all."

But Moses begged the LORD his God not to do it. So the LORD stopped. He didn't bring disaster against his people.

Then Moses went down the mountain. He held in his hands the two stone tablets carved with the words written by God himself.

When he came near the camp, Moses smashed the tablets on the ground in terrible anger. He took the calf they had made and melted it in the fire. And when the metal had cooled, he ground it into powder and mixed it with water. Then he made the people drink it.

Story based on Exodus 32:1-20 as it appears in the New Living Translation®.

Let's talk about it...

Aaron knew that it was wrong to make and worship an idol, but he went along with the crowd. As Aaron found out, it's hard to be the only one saying NO. Maybe your friends have tried to get you to cheat on a test or get into a movie that is off-limits. That's when we can think about what God wants us to do and follow him instead of the crowd.

My child, if sinners entice you, turn your back on them!
Proverbs 1:10, NLT

Too Scared to Go

Walking into a new classroom can be scary. Will the teacher be nice? How will your classmates treat you? The Israelites were scared about entering the new land God had promised them.

See what happened to them...

The LORD said to Moses, "Send one leader from each of the twelve tribes to explore Canaan."

Moses gave the leaders these instructions: "See what the land is like and find out whether the people living there are strong or weak, few or many. Enter the land bravely, and bring back samples of the food."

After exploring the land for forty days, the men returned and said: "The land of Canaan is indeed wonderful. The people living there are powerful, and their cities and towns are large and well protected."

But Caleb tried to cheer the people, saying, "Let's go at once to take the land."

But the other men who had explored the land with him were afraid. They said scary things. Then all the people began crying. Their voices rose in a great chorus of complaint against Moses and Aaron. They even talked about choosing a new leader so they could go back to Egypt!

Two of the explorers, Joshua and Caleb, said, "The land we explored is a great place! If the LORD is pleased with us, he'll bring us into that land safely."

But the whole community began to talk about stoning Joshua and Caleb. Then the LORD said to Moses,

"How long will these people turn against me? I will turn against them and destroy them."

"Please, LORD, prove that your power is as great as you have claimed. Forgive the sins of these people because your love never fails," Moses said.

Then the LORD said, "I will forgive them as you asked. But none of those who have treated me this way will enter the land. However, my servant Caleb has stayed loyal to me. I will bring him into the land he explored."

Story based on Numbers 13:1–14:24 as it appears in the New Living Translation®.

Let's talk about it...

When the Israelites heard the reports about the new land, they focused on all the bad things, and they let their fears stop them. When we're in a new and scary situation, we can let our fears stop us. Or we can trust in God's promises to be with us and guide us. Which do you choose?

I will not be afraid, for you are close beside me.
Psalm 23:4, NLT

The Secret to Success

What does it take to be successful? Some might say hard work, others might say luck. But for God's people, there's only one requirement—obedience. God's people, Israel, needed a new leader.

Discover what God promises Israel as Joshua takes charge...

After the death of Moses the LORD's servant, the LORD spoke to Joshua, Moses' helper. He said, "You must lead my people into the land I am giving them. I promise you what I promised Moses: 'Everywhere you go, you will be standing on land I have given you.' For I will be with you as I was with Moses. I will not fail you or leave you.

"Be strong and brave, for you will lead my people to take all the land I promised to give their ancestors. Obey all the laws Moses gave you, and you will be successful in everything you do. Do not be afraid. Don't give up. For the LORD your God is with you wherever you go."

Joshua then commanded the leaders of Israel, "Go through the camp and tell the people to get ready. In three days you will cross the Jordan River and take over the land God has given you."

Then Joshua called together the tribes of Reuben, Gad, and Manasseh. He told them, "Remember what Moses, the servant of the LORD, commanded you. Your warriors, fully armed, must lead the other tribes across the Jordan to help them take their land. Only then may

you live here on the east side of the Jordan River in the land that Moses, the servant of the LORD, gave you."

They answered Joshua, "We will do whatever you command us. We will obey you just as we obeyed Moses. And may the LORD your God be with you as he was with Moses. So be strong and brave!"

Story based on Joshua 1:1-18 as it appears in the New Living Translation®.

Let's talk about it...

Did you catch what God said? *"Obey all the laws Moses gave you. . . . Only then will you succeed."* God promises success to those who know his Word and obey it. God also promises to be with us as long as we obey him. Seems pretty simple, doesn't it? Obey God, and you will succeed. How can we practice that today? God promises to help!

> But I lavish my love on those who love me
> and obey my commands.
> *Exodus 20:6, NLT*

Rahab's Risk

Joshua secretly sent out two spies and told them, "Spy out the land on the other side of the Jordan River, especially around Jericho." So the two men set out and came to the house of Rahab, a prostitute.

Someone told the king of Jericho, "Some Israelite spies have come here." So the king sent orders to Rahab: "Bring out the men who have come to you."

Rahab, who had hidden the two men on her roof, said, "The men were here earlier, but I didn't know where they were from. I don't know where they went, but if you hurry, you can probably catch them." So the king's men went looking for the spies.

Rahab went up on the roof to talk with the spies. "I know the LORD has given you this land," she told them. "We are all afraid of you. For the LORD your God is the highest God. Now promise me by the LORD that you will be kind to me and my family since I helped you."

Then Rahab let them down by a rope through the window. Before they left, the men told her, "We can promise you safety only if you leave this scarlet rope hanging from the window. We promise that no one inside this house will be killed. If you turn against us, however, we don't have to keep our promise."

Then the spies went up into the hill country and stayed there three days. They returned to Joshua and told all that had happened. "The LORD will certainly give us the whole land," they said, "for all the people in the land are terrified of us."

Story based on Joshua 2:1-24 as it appears in the New Living Translation®.

Let's talk about it...

It was dangerous for Rahab to help enemy spies. But she was willing to take that risk because she wanted to obey God. Obeying God can be risky business. It might mean being teased because you won't watch a certain TV show or being the only one to tell the truth. But, like Rahab, you can trust that when you obey God, he will take care of you.

For the LORD protects those who are loyal to him.
Psalm 31:23, NLT

God's Strange Battle Plan

Sometimes you get instructions that just don't make sense. You can either follow the instructions, or come up with your own plan. In this story God gave the people some very strange rules to capture a city.
Look at what they did...

Now the gates of Jericho were tightly shut because the people were afraid of the Israelites. But the LORD said to Joshua, "I have given you Jericho, its king, and all its mighty warriors. Your whole army is to march around the city once a day for six days. Seven priests will walk ahead of the ark of the covenant, each carrying a ram's horn. On the seventh day you are to march around the city seven times, with the priests blowing the horns. When the priests give one long blast on the horns, have all the people give a mighty shout. Then the walls of the city will fall down, and the people can charge into the city."

So Joshua called together the priests and the people to give them the orders of the LORD. After Joshua spoke to them, they obeyed the LORD's command. They followed this pattern for six days.

On the seventh day, the Israelites got up early. But this time they went around the city seven times. The seventh time around, as the priests sounded the long blast on their horns, Joshua commanded the people, "Shout! For the LORD has given you the city! The city and everything in it must be completely destroyed as

an offering to the LORD. Only Rahab and the others in her house will be saved, because she kept our spies safe."

When the people heard the sound of the horns, they shouted as loudly as they could. Suddenly, the walls of Jericho fell down, and the Israelites charged straight into the city from every side and captured it.

Story based on Joshua 6:1-20 as it appears in the New Living Translation®.

Let's talk about it...

It was good that the Israelites followed God's instructions, wasn't it? The Israelites might have thought God's orders were strange, but they trusted God, obeyed him anyway, and won the battle! God gives us instructions, too, from his Word and through other people. When we follow God's directions, amazing things can—and will—happen.

Those who obey God's commandments
live in fellowship with him, and he with them.
I John 3:24, NLT

A Tough Assignment

What do you do when you face a big chore at home or a hard assignment at school? Do you jump right in, ready to take it on? Or do you wait for help? Barak faced a tough assignment.
Examine how he handled it...

The Israelites again did what was evil in the LORD's sight. So the LORD handed them over to King Jabin of Hazor, a Canaanite king. Sisera, the commander of Jabin's army, mistreated the Israelites for twenty years. Then the Israelites cried out to the LORD.

Deborah, a prophet and judge in Israel, held court under the Palm of Deborah. She settled the disagreements of the Israelites. One day she told Barak, "This is what the LORD commands you: Get ten thousand warriors ready. I will have Sisera and his army go to the Kishon River and give you victory."

Barak told her, "I will only go if you go with me!"

"Very well," she said, "But since you have made this choice, you will receive no honor. The LORD's victory over Sisera will be at the hands of a woman."

Then Deborah said to Barak, "Get ready! Today the LORD will give you victory over Sisera. The LORD is marching ahead of you." So Barak led his ten thousand warriors into battle. When Barak attacked, the LORD threw Sisera and all his warriors into a panic. Then Sisera leaped down from his chariot and escaped, but not one of Sisera's warriors was left alive.

Meanwhile, Sisera ran to the tent of Jael because her family was friendly with King Jabin. Jael said, "Come into my tent, sir." So he went into her tent.

Sisera was very tired. When he fell asleep, Jael quietly crept up to him and drove a tent peg through his head and into the ground. So he died.

So on that day Israel saw God win over the Canaanites.

Story based on Judges 4:1-23 as it appears in the New Living Translation®.

Let's talk about it...

Barak and Deborah had the same task—defeat Sisera. Deborah was ready to march into battle. Barak wanted more help. What was the difference in their responses? Faith. Deborah believed that God would win the battle. When we have a tough job to do, we can either rely on God's help or wait for more help. Will you have faith like Deborah?

Some nations boast of their armies and weapons, but we boast in the LORD, our God.
Psalm 20:7, NLT

Going Against the Odds

Would your soccer team play against the best team in town with only half a team? Probably not. Your team wouldn't stand a chance. But God sent Gideon to fight thousands of Midianites with only 300 men.
Find out what happened...

Gideon and his army got up early to fight the armies of Midian. The LORD said to Gideon, "If I let all of you fight the Midianites, the Israelites will brag to me that they saved themselves. Tell anyone who is afraid to go home." Twenty-two thousand went home, leaving only ten thousand to fight.

But the LORD told Gideon, "There are still too many! Bring them down to the spring and have the men drink." They did. Then the LORD told Gideon, "With the three hundred men who drank from their hands, I will rescue you."

During the night, the LORD said, "If you are afraid to attack, go to the camp and listen to the Midianites."

So Gideon and his servant, Purah, went to the enemy camp. Gideon heard a warrior saying, "In my dream a loaf of barley bread came tumbling down into the Midianite camp. It hit a tent, turned it over, and knocked it flat!"

His friend said, "Your dream can mean only one thing—God has given Gideon victory!"

When Gideon heard this, he thanked God. Then he returned to the Israelite camp and shouted, "The LORD has given you victory over the Midianites! Watch me and do just as I do."

Just after midnight Gideon and his men reached the Midianite camp. They blew the horns and broke their clay jars. They shouted, "A sword for the LORD and for Gideon!" When they blew their horns, the LORD caused the warriors in the camp to fight against each other. Some of them killed each other. The others ran away.

Story based on Judges 7:1-22 as it appears in the New Living Translation®.

Let's talk about it...

God didn't just want to help Gideon's army win. God wanted the victory to show everyone his power. If Gideon's army had been huge, the soldiers would have taken the credit. But since Gideon's army was small and weak, they *needed* God to win. When we feel small and weak, we find out how super powerful God is—no matter the odds!

Nothing can hinder the LORD.
1 Samuel 14:6, NLT

Samson Makes a Bad Choice

What kind of friends do you have? Friends that help you do the right thing, or friends that steer you in a wrong direction? Samson had to choose between obeying God and doing what his girlfriend wanted.

Look at what Samson chose...

Samson fell in love with a woman named Delilah. The leaders of the Philistines offered her money to find out what made Samson so strong.

So Delilah said to Samson, "Please tell me what makes you so strong. What would it take to tie you up tight?" But Samson would not tell Delilah.

So day after day Delilah nagged Samson until he couldn't stand it any longer. Finally, Samson told her his secret: "My hair has never been cut, for I was dedicated to God as a Nazirite from birth. If my head were shaved, my strength would leave me."

Delilah knew he had finally told her the truth, so she sent for the Philistines. Delilah lulled Samson to sleep and called in a man to shave off his hair.

When Samson woke up, he thought, "I will shake myself free." But he didn't know the LORD had left him. So the Philistines captured him and gouged out his eyes. They put bronze chains on him and made him grind grain in the prison. But before long his hair began to grow back.

The Philistine leaders held a great festival. Samson was brought from the prison and made to stand at the

center of the temple. He stood between the two pillars that held up the roof.

Then Samson prayed to the LORD, "O God, please strengthen me one more time so that I may pay back the Philistines for the loss of my eyes." Then Samson pushed against the pillars with all his might. And the temple crashed down on the Philistines. So he killed many of God's enemies when he died.

Story based on Judges 16:4-30 as it appears in the New Living Translation®.

Let's talk about it...

Samson chose poorly when he made Delilah his girlfriend. He did what she wanted instead of obeying God. Choosing whom to spend time with can be hard. Some friends make it easier to obey your parents. Other friends may try to get you to take someone else's lunch, or spread rumors about another friend. Which type of friend do you choose?

A real friend sticks closer than a brother.
Proverbs 18:24, NLT

A True Friend

What kind of friend are you? Do you stick by a friend in good times *and* in bad times? That's what we call being loyal. Having loyal friends is extra important when we face tough situations.

Check out what kind of friend Ruth is...

A man named Elimelech left Bethlehem because there was no food. He took his wife, Naomi, and two sons and went to live in Moab. During their stay in Moab, Elimelech died and Naomi was left with her two sons. The two sons married Moabite women named Orpah and Ruth. But ten years later, both sons died. This left Naomi with only her daughters-in-law.

Then Naomi heard that the LORD had blessed his people in Judah by giving them good crops again. So Naomi and her daughters-in-law got ready to return to her homeland. But on the way, Naomi said to Orpah and Ruth, "Go back to your mothers' homes." Then she kissed them good-bye, and they all cried.

Orpah kissed Naomi good-bye. But Ruth insisted on staying with Naomi, saying "Don't ask me to leave you and turn back. I will go wherever you go and live wherever you live. Your people will be my people, and your God will be my God."

So Naomi and Ruth arrived in Bethlehem. One day Ruth said to Naomi, "Let me go out into the fields to gather leftover grain."

And Naomi said, "All right, go ahead." While Ruth was working in Boaz's field, Boaz asked one of his

workers, "Who is that girl over there?" And the worker said, "She is the young woman from Moab who came back with Naomi. She has been working very hard."

Boaz went over and said to Ruth, "Listen, my daughter. Stay here with us when you gather grain. I will protect you."

Ruth fell at his feet and thanked him. "Why are you so kind to me?" she asked. Boaz answered, "I know about the kindness you have shown Naomi since the death of your husband. The LORD will reward you."

Story based on Ruth 1:1-2:12 as it appears in the New Living Translation®.

Let's talk about it...

It was hard for Ruth to leave her home to go with Naomi. But God rewarded Ruth's kindness in many ways. She found food, a new home, and even a new husband. That's the kind of friend God wants us to be— a friend who will be there whatever happens. What friends need you to be loyal to them right now?

A friend is always loyal.
Proverbs 17:17, NLT

Are You Listening?

How good are you at listening? In this story young Samuel heard someone calling his name. It took Samuel a while to figure out who was really trying to get his attention.

Discover whose voice was calling in the night...

The boy Samuel was serving the LORD by helping Eli. Now in those days messages from the LORD were very unusual, and so were visions.

One night Eli had just gone to bed, and Samuel was sleeping near the ark of God. Suddenly, the LORD called out, "Samuel! Samuel!"

"Yes?" Samuel replied. "What is it?" He jumped up and ran to Eli. "Here I am. What do you need?"

"I didn't call you," Eli replied. "Go on back to bed."

This happened twice more until Eli realized it was the LORD who was calling the boy. So he said to Samuel, "Go and lie down again, and if someone calls again, say, 'Yes, LORD, your servant is listening.'" So Samuel went back to bed.

And the LORD came and called as before. And Samuel replied, "Yes, your servant is listening."

Then the LORD said to Samuel, "I have warned Eli that judgment is coming for his family. His sons are doing wrong to God, and Eli hasn't made them behave well. So I have promised that the sins of Eli and his sons will never be forgiven by sacrifices or offerings."

Samuel stayed in bed until morning, then got up and opened the doors of the tabernacle as usual. He was

afraid to tell Eli what the LORD said. But Eli called out to him, "Samuel, my son. What did the LORD say to you? Tell me everything." So Samuel did. "It is the LORD's will," Eli answered. "Let him do what is best."

As Samuel grew up, the LORD was with him, and everything Samuel said was true. All the people of Israel knew that Samuel was a prophet of the LORD.

Story based on 1 Samuel 3:1-20 as it appears in the New Living Translation®.

Let's talk about it...

God was calling to Samuel, but Samuel didn't recognize God's voice. Samuel wasn't expecting God to speak out loud. Maybe you've never heard God speak to you out loud. But God can give us messages in lots of ways. He might speak to us through parents, a preacher, a teacher, or a friend. God also talks to us when we read the Bible. Are you listening?

But God speaks again and again,
though people do not recognize it.
Job 33:14, NLT

We Want a King!

What was the last thing you really wanted because everyone else had it? Maybe it was a pair of gym shoes, the coolest jeans, or a new CD. In this story the Israelites wanted to be like everyone else too.

Read what happens...

As Samuel grew old, he chose his sons to be judges over Israel. But they were not like their father, for they were greedy for money.

Finally, the leaders of Israel met at Ramah to talk about it with Samuel. "Look," they told him, "you are now old, and your sons are not like you. Give us a king like all the other nations have."

Samuel was very upset with their request and went to the LORD for advice. "Do as they say," the LORD answered, "for it is me they are rejecting, not you. Ever since I brought them from Egypt they keep leaving me to follow other gods. Do as they ask, but warn them about how a king will treat them."

So Samuel passed on the LORD's warning to the people. But the people refused to listen to Samuel's warning. "Even so, we still want a king," they said. "We want to be like the nations around us. Our king will rule us and lead us into battle."

So the LORD told Samuel, "Do as they say, and give them a king." Later Samuel called the tribal leaders together before the LORD. And finally Saul son of Kish was chosen from among them to be king. But when

they looked for him, he had disappeared! So they asked the LORD, "Where is he?"

And the LORD replied, "He is hiding with the baggage." So they found him and brought him out.

Then Samuel said to all the people, "This is the man the LORD has chosen as your king. No one in all Israel is like him!"

Story based on 1 Samuel 8:1-22; 10:20-24 as it appears in the New Living Translation®.

Let's talk about it...

Having a king didn't sound so great, but the Israelites didn't care. They wanted to be just like all the other nations. Sometimes wanting to be like everyone else can cause us to make wrong choices. That's when we need to stop and listen to what God tells us is right for us instead of trying to be like a friend or classmate.

But my people would not listen to me.
They kept on doing whatever they wanted,
following the stubborn desires of their evil hearts.
Jeremiah 7:24, NLT

No Time to Panic

When you face a scary situation or a tough job, what do you do? Sometimes it's easy to panic and make the wrong decision. When Saul saw a mighty army getting ready to attack the Israelites, he panicked. *See what happens as a result...*

Saul chose three thousand special soldiers from the army of Israel and sent the rest of the men home. He took two thousand of the soldiers with him, and the other thousand went with Saul's son Jonathan.

Soon after this, Jonathan attacked the Philistines at Geba and won. The news spread quickly among the Philistines that Israel was planning attacks. Saul warned the people that the Philistines now hated the Israelites more than ever.

The Philistines gathered a mighty army. When the men of Israel saw the large number of enemy soldiers, they were very afraid and tried to hide.

Meanwhile, Saul stayed at Gilgal, and his men were trembling with fear. Saul waited there seven days for Samuel, but Samuel still didn't come. So Saul sacrificed a burnt offering himself. Just as Saul was finishing with the burnt offering, Samuel arrived. Saul went out to meet and welcome him, but Samuel said, "What is this you have done?"

Saul answered, "I saw my men scattering from me, and you didn't arrive when you said you would. The Philistines are ready for battle. So I felt I had to offer the burnt offering myself before you came."

"How foolish!" Samuel exclaimed. "You have disobeyed the command of the LORD your God. Had you obeyed, the LORD would have kept your kingdom over Israel forever. But the LORD has already chosen a man after his own heart to be king over his people, for you have not obeyed the LORD's command."

Story based on 1 Samuel 13:2-14 as it appears in the New Living Translation®.

Let's talk about it...

Saul and his men were so scared that they started imagining the worst. They forgot about trusting in God. Sometimes we get really scared too. We may think about all the bad things that could happen. When that happens we need to remember that God is always with us. God can help us in any situation—no matter how scary it seems.

Though the wicked hide along the way to kill me,
I will quietly keep my mind on your decrees.
Psalm 119:95, NLT

Is That What a King Looks Like?

An impression is what we remember about a person. It could be how a person looks, or what she is wearing, or what he can do. Samuel had some strong impressions about the people in this story.
But look at what impresses God...

The LORD said to Samuel, "I have rejected Saul as king of Israel. Now fill a horn with olive oil and go to Bethlehem. Find a man named Jesse who lives there, for I have chosen one of his sons to be my new king."

So Samuel did as the LORD told him. When he arrived at Bethlehem, he said, "Purify yourselves and come to the sacrifice." Then Samuel helped Jesse and his sons purify themselves and invited them too.

When they arrived, Samuel took one look at Eliab and thought, "Surely this is the LORD's chosen one!" But the LORD said to Samuel, "Don't judge by his appearance or height, for I have rejected him. The LORD doesn't make decisions the way you do! People judge by outward appearance, but the LORD looks at a person's thoughts and heart."

In the same way all seven of Jesse's sons were presented to Samuel. But Samuel said to Jesse, "The LORD has not chosen any of these. Are these all the sons you have?"

"There is still the youngest," Jesse replied. "But he's out in the fields watching the sheep."

"Send for him at once," Samuel said. "We will not sit down to eat until he arrives."

So Jesse sent for him. He was handsome, with pleasant eyes. And the LORD said, "Anoint him."

So as David stood there among his brothers, Samuel poured the olive oil on David's head. And the Spirit of the LORD came mightily upon him from that day on.

Story based on 1 Samuel 16:1-13 as it appears in the New Living Translation®.

Let's talk about it...

When Samuel saw Eliab, he was sure that God would make Eliab king. But God wasn't impressed with Eliab's appearance. God was looking at how Eliab thought and acted. That's how God wants us to look at each other. It doesn't matter what a person looks like or wears. What's most important is what's on the inside—a person's heart and mind.

As a face is reflected in water,
so the heart reflects the person.
Proverbs 27:19, NLT

A Giant Problem

What's the biggest problem you've had? How did you handle it? Maybe you ignored it, ran away from it, or faced it. In this story the Israelites had a GIANT problem. And only one young boy knew the solution. Discover what he knew...

David set out to take gifts to his brothers, who were with Saul's army. He saw Goliath come out from the Philistine side, shouting a dare to the army of Israel. When the Israelites saw him, they ran in fear.

Then the king sent for David. "Don't worry about a thing," David told Saul. "I'll go fight this Philistine!"

"Don't be ridiculous!" Saul replied. "You are only a boy, and he has been in the army since he was a boy!"

But David wouldn't give up. "When a lion or a bear comes to steal a lamb from the flock, I go after it with a club and take the lamb from its mouth. The LORD who saved me from the claws of the lion and the bear will save me from this Philistine!"

Saul finally agreed. "All right, go ahead," he said. "And may the LORD be with you!"

So David picked up five smooth stones from a stream and put them in his shepherd's bag. Then, with his stick and sling, he went to fight Goliath.

Goliath walked out toward David, making fun of the boy. "Come over here, and I'll give your body to the birds and wild animals!" Goliath yelled.

David shouted back, "You come to me with sword, spear, and javelin, but I come to you in the name of

the L ORD Almighty. Today the L ORD will win, and I will kill you and cut off your head."

As Goliath moved to attack, David ran out to meet him. He hurled a stone from his sling and hit Goliath in the forehead. The stone sank in, and Goliath fell facedown. David ran over, pulled out Goliath's sword, and used it to kill the giant and cut off his head.

Story based on 1 Samuel 17:19-51 as it appears in the New Living Translation®.

Let's talk about it...

The Israelites had a GIANT problem, but David wasn't afraid. He knew that God was more powerful than Goliath. God was on David's side, and he is on our side too! God can help us overcome all kinds of giant problems—big bullies, tough teachers, or hard homework. No problem is too big for God.

Some nations boast of their armies and weapons, but we boast in the L ORD our God.
Psalm 20:7, NLT

A Forever Friendship

Best friends are great. Maybe you have had the same best friend as long as you can remember. In this story David and Saul's son Jonathan become very good friends.

Find out what kept these best friends together...

David became best friends with Jonathan, the king's son. One day David found Jonathan and asked, "What have I done that your father has decided to kill me?"

Jonathan said, "Oh, no, I'm sure he's not planning any such thing. I know he wouldn't hide this from me."

Then David said, "Your father has said to himself, 'I won't tell Jonathan—why should I hurt him?' But I'm telling you the truth. I'm only a step away from death!"

"Tell me what I can do!" Jonathan exclaimed.

David answered, "I always eat with Saul at the festival, but tomorrow I'll hide in the field until the third day. If he asks where I am, tell him I asked to go home for a family sacrifice. If he says, 'Fine!' all is well. But if he gets angry, you'll know he plans to kill me."

When the festival began, Saul asked Jonathan, "Why hasn't David been here for dinner?"

Jonathan answered, "David asked me if he could take part in a family sacrifice. I told him to go."

Saul boiled with anger at Jonathan. He yelled. "As long as David lives, you'll never be king. Go get him so I can kill him!"

As David and Jonathan had planned, Jonathan went out to the field with a young boy to gather the arrows

he shot. "Start running," he told the boy, and then shot an arrow beyond him. Jonathan shouted, "The arrow is still ahead of you. Hurry, hurry, don't wait."

When the boy was gone, David came out from hiding. Both David and Jonathan were in tears as they hugged and said good-bye. At last Jonathan said, "Go in peace. We will trust God. We will place each other and each other's children into God's hands."

Story based on 1 Samuel 18:1-3; 20:1-42 as it appears in the New Living Translation®.

Let's talk about it...

God showed Jonathan how to be a good friend by helping keep David safe. Even though David had to leave, he and Jonathan knew that God would keep their friendship strong. When friends love God and each other, their friendship will last. Have you asked God to be part of your friendships?

Dear friends, let us continue to love one another, for love comes from God.

1 John 4:7, NLT

Love Your Enemies?

What if the kid who's always making fun of you tripped and fell right in the middle of the cafeteria? Would you point and laugh, or would you help him up? David had a chance to get back at his enemy.

Check out how David used that opportunity...

Saul chose three thousand special soldiers and went to search for David and his men. Saul went by himself into a cave. But as it happened, David and his men were hiding there!

"Now's your chance!" David's men whispered to him. "Today is the day the LORD was talking about when he said, 'I will certainly put Saul into your power, to do with as you wish.'" Then David crept forward and cut off a piece of Saul's robe.

But David's heart began bothering him because he had cut Saul's robe. "It is a serious thing to attack the LORD's chosen one," David said. So David scolded his men and did not let them kill Saul.

After Saul had left the cave, David came out and shouted after him, "My lord the king!" And when Saul looked around, David bowed low before him.

Then he shouted to Saul, "Why do you listen to the people who say I am trying to harm you? This very day you can see with your own eyes it isn't true. Look, my father, at what I have in my hand. It is a piece of your robe! I cut it off, but I didn't kill you. This proves that I am not trying to harm you. I have not sinned against you, even though you have been trying to kill me."

Saul called back, "Is that really you, my son David?" Then he began to cry. And he said to David, "You are a better man than I am, for you have repaid me good for evil. And now I understand that you are surely going to be king. Israel will do well under your rule."

Story based on 1 Samuel 24:1-20 as it appears in the New Living Translation®.

Let's talk about it...

Even though Saul wanted to kill David, David didn't hurt Saul. And Saul's attitude changed when David showed him kindness. When someone always hurts us or calls us names, it's really hard to be kind to that person. It's not easy to love our enemies. But loving our enemies could make all the difference. Try it!

But I say, love your enemies!
Pray for those who persecute you!
Matthew 5:44, NLT

God Makes David King

What does it take to be a king, or a powerful leader, or even a good student? You may be surprised at the answer found in this story.

Listen as God tells King David about how he became king...

Then all the tribes of Israel went to David and told him, "For a long time, even while Saul was our king, you were the one who really led Israel. And the LORD has told you, 'You will be the shepherd of my people Israel. You will be their leader.'" So David made an agreement with the leaders of Israel before the LORD. And they anointed him king of Israel.

Then the LORD said to Nathan, the prophet, "Now go and say to my servant David, 'This is what the LORD Almighty says: I chose you to lead my people Israel when you were just a shepherd boy. I have been with you wherever you have gone, and I have destroyed all your enemies. Now I will make your name famous throughout the earth! And I have wonderful land where my people Israel can live, a safe place where they will never be harmed. I will keep you safe from all your enemies.

"'And now the LORD says that he will build a house for you—a dynasty of kings! For when you die, I will raise up one of your descendants, and I will make his kingdom strong. He is the one who will build a house— a temple—for my name. And I will keep the throne of his kingdom forever. I will be his father, and he will be

my son. If he sins, I will use other nations to punish him. But my love will not be taken from him as I took it from Saul. Your dynasty and your kingdom will continue for all time before me. Your throne will be in place forever.'"

Story based on 2 Samuel 5:1-5; 7:8-16 as it appears in the New Living Translation®.

Let's talk about it...

David didn't have to be super-smart or take classes to be king. From the beginning, God planned for David to be king. All David had to do was trust God and obey him. God has wonderful and exciting plans for each of us. It doesn't matter if you're not the smartest, or the fastest, or the most talented. If you trust God and obey him, God can do it!

"For I know the plans I have for you," says the LORD. "They are plans for good and not for disaster, to give you a future and a hope."

Jeremiah 29:11, NLT

David the Promise-Keeper

Keeping promises is very important. When someone breaks a promise, it's hard to trust that person again. In this story David honors an old promise he made. Look at what happens when David keeps his word...

One day David began wondering if anyone in Saul's family was still alive. He had promised Jonathan that he would show kindness to them. He called a man named Ziba, who had been one of Saul's servants.

The king then asked him, "Is anyone still alive from Saul's family?"

Ziba replied, "Yes, one of Jonathan's sons is still alive, but he is disabled."

So David sent for him. His name was Mephibosheth; he was Jonathan's son and Saul's grandson. When he came to David, he bowed low in great fear and said, "I am your servant."

But David said, "Don't be afraid! I've asked you to come so that I can be kind to you because of my promise to your father, Jonathan. I will give you all the land that once belonged to your grandfather Saul, and you may live here with me at the palace!"

Mephibosheth fell to the ground before the king. "Should the king show such kindness to a dead dog like me?" he exclaimed.

And from that time on, Mephibosheth always ate with David, as though he were one of his own sons. Mephibosheth had a young son named Mica. And from then on, all the members of Ziba's household

were Mephibosheth's servants. And Mephibosheth, who was disabled in both feet, moved to Jerusalem to live at the palace.

Story based on 2 Samuel 9:1-13 as it appears in the New Living Translation®.

Let's talk about it...

It had been years since David made the promise to Jonathan. No one else remembered the promise, but it was important to David to keep his word. God always keeps his promises, and he wants us to do the same. When we make a promise, our family and friends depend on us to keep it. Is anyone waiting for you to keep a promise?

The LORD hates those who don't keep their word, but he delights in those who do.
Proverbs 12:22, NLT

King David's Tough Lesson

When a brother or sister does something wrong, do you run to tell your parents about it? What about when you do something wrong? It's much harder to admit our own mistakes.

King David discovers that for himself...

The LORD sent Nathan the prophet to tell David this story: "There were two men in a certain town. One was rich, and one was poor. The poor man owned nothing but a little lamb he had worked hard to buy. He raised that little lamb, and it grew up with his children. It ate from the man's own plate and drank from his cup. He cuddled it in his arms like a baby. One day a guest arrived at the home of the rich man. But instead of killing a lamb from his own flocks, he took the poor man's lamb and killed it and served it to his guest."

David was very angry. "As surely as the LORD lives," he promised, "any man who would do such a thing should die! He must repay four lambs to the poor man for the one he stole. He didn't feel sorry at all."

Then Nathan said to David, "You are that man! The LORD says, 'I chose you to be king and saved you from Saul. I gave you what was Saul's and the kingdoms of Israel and Judah. And if that had not been enough, I would have given you much, much more. Why, then, have you disobeyed the word of the LORD? You murdered Uriah and stole his wife. From now on there will be people in your family who are killed with swords. That is because you did not respect the LORD.'"

Then David confessed to Nathan, "I have sinned against the LORD." Nathan answered, "Yes, but the LORD has forgiven you, and you won't die for this sin. But you have given the enemies of the LORD a chance to disrespect him, so your child will die."

Story based on 2 Samuel 12:1-14 as it appears in the New Living Translation®.

Let's talk about it...

It's easy to see when other people do something wrong. But as David found out in the story, it's often difficult to see and admit our own mistakes. That's why we need to look at our own thoughts and actions before pointing at others. When we do wrong things, follow David. Admit them, and ask God for forgiveness.

First get rid of the log from your own eye; then perhaps you will see well enough to deal with the speck in your friend's eye.

Matthew 7:5, NLT

David's Family Feud

Families can be great—and sometimes, not so great. When everyone gets along, family life is wonderful. But when there's fighting and arguing, family life is tough. King David had lots of family trouble.

Check it out...

A messenger arrived in Jerusalem to tell King David, "All Israel has joined your son Absalom against you!"

"Then we must get away at once, or it will be too late!" David told his men. So David chose generals and captains to lead his soldiers. The king told his soldiers, "I am going with you."

But his men said, "Oh, no! You must not go. You are worth ten thousand of us. It is better for you to stay here and send help if we need it."

"If you think that's the best plan, I'll do it," the king finally agreed. And the king gave this command to Joab, Abishai, and Ittai: "For my sake, be gentle with young Absalom." And all the soldiers heard this order.

During the battle, Absalom tried to escape on his mule, but his head got caught in the branches of a tree. His mule kept going and left him dangling. One of David's men saw what had happened and told Joab.

"What?" Joab demanded. "I would have rewarded you with ten pieces of silver and a hero's belt if you had killed him!"

"I wouldn't do it for a thousand pieces of silver," the man replied. "We all heard the king say, 'For my sake, please don't harm young Absalom.'"

Then Joab took three spears and plunged them into Absalom's heart as he dangled from the oak. Then Joab's young armor bearers killed Absalom.

The king was overcome with emotion. He went up to his room and burst into tears. And as he went, he cried, "O my son, Absalom! If only I could have died instead of you! O Absalom, my son, my son."

Story based on 2 Samuel 15:13, 14; 18:1-33 as it appears in the New Living Translation®.

Let's talk about it...

When Absalom died, David was very sad. Family fights make God sad too. God wants families to help each other and love each other. Next time a family fight is brewing, remember God's plan. Instead of joining the fight, be the peacemaker in your family.

How wonderful it is, how pleasant,
when brothers live together in harmony!
Psalm 133:1, NLT

Solomon's Wise Wish

What if God offered to give you anything you wanted in this entire world? What would you ask for? God gave King Solomon an opportunity to have anything he wanted.

Read to uncover Solomon's great wish...

King Solomon loved the LORD. One night the LORD appeared to Solomon in a dream, and God said, "What do you want? Ask, and I will give it to you!"

Solomon answered, "Give me understanding so that I can know the difference between right and wrong. For who is able to rule this great nation by himself?"

The LORD was pleased and said, "I will give you a wise and understanding mind such as no one else has ever had! And I will also give you riches and honor! And if you follow me, I will give you a long life."

Some time later, two women came to the king to have an argument settled. One of them began, "This woman and I live together. Her baby died during the night. Then she got up and took my son from beside me while I was asleep."

Then the other woman interrupted, "The living child is mine."

"No," the first woman said, "the dead one is yours, and the living one is mine." And so they argued.

The king said, "All right, bring a sword. Cut the living child in two and give half to each woman!"

Then the woman who really was the mother of the living child cried out, "Oh no, my lord! Give her the child—please do not kill him!"

But the other woman did not care about the child.

So Solomon said, "Do not kill him. Give the baby to the woman who wants him to live. She is his mother!"

This news spread quickly. The people thought the great wisdom God had given Solomon was awesome.

Story based on 1 Kings 3:3-28 as it appears in the New Living Translation®.

Let's talk about it...

When King Solomon asked God for wisdom, God was so pleased that he gave him riches and honor too. Wisdom is more than just being smart or knowing a lot of stuff. Wisdom helps us see what is best and shows us how God wants us to live. When you don't know what to do, ask God. He wants to give you wisdom.

If you need wisdom—if you want to know what God wants you to do—ask him, and he will gladly tell you.

James 1:5, NLT

Rehoboam's Tough Act

Who's the toughest kid in your school? Sometimes kids (and even adults) act tough because they want to impress others. That's usually not a good way to make friends. See what happens when Rehoboam acts tough...

The people of Israel went to speak with King Rehoboam. "Your father made us work very hard," they said. "Make it easier on us. Then we will be loyal to you."

Then King Rehoboam went to talk about this with the older men who had helped his father, Solomon. "What is your advice?" he asked.

The older counselors replied, "If you are willing to serve the people today and give them a good answer, they will always be loyal."

But Rehoboam didn't like the advice of the elders, so he asked the advice of the young men who were now his advisers.

The young men replied, "This is what you should tell those complainers: 'Yes, my father was hard on you, but I'll be even harder!'"

Three days later, Jeroboam and all the people returned to hear Rehoboam's decision. But Rehoboam spoke harshly to them, for he didn't take the advice of the older counselors. He followed the ideas of his younger advisers.

When Israel saw that the king wouldn't do what they asked, they shouted, "Down with David's family!"

King Rehoboam sent Adoniram, who was in charge of the workers. But all Israel stoned him to death. When King Rehoboam heard this, he quickly jumped

into his chariot and ran away to Jerusalem. From then on the northern tribes of Israel have to be ruled by a descendant of David. Only the tribe of Judah remained loyal to the family of David.

Story based on 1 Kings 12:3-20 as it appears in the New Living Translation®.

Let's talk about it...

Rehoboam would have been much more successful if he had listened to the older advisers and treated the people kindly and fairly. Then the people would have been glad to have him as their king. Being a tough guy did not make Rehoboam popular. The best way to treat other people is the way we want to be treated.

Do for others as you would like them to do for you.
Luke 6:31, NLT

God's Special Delivery

Can you imagine not having any rain for three years? God withheld the rain that long to get the attention of wicked King Ahab. It was hard for anyone to live during this time, but God took special care of Elijah.

Find out how God cared for Elijah...

Ahab ruled in Samaria twenty-two years. But Ahab did what was evil in the LORD's sight, even more than any of the kings before him. It was bad enough to be evil like Jeroboam. But Ahab also married Jezebel, and he began to worship Jezebel's false god, Baal. First he built a temple and an altar for Baal in Samaria. Then he set up an Asherah pole, a carved wooden idol used to worship another false god. He did more to anger the LORD, the God of Israel, than any of the other kings of Israel before him.

Now Elijah, who was a prophet, told King Ahab, "As surely as the LORD, the God of Israel, lives—the God whom I worship and serve—there will be no dew or rain during the next few years unless I give the word!"

Then the LORD said to Elijah, "Go to the east and hide by Kerith Brook at a place east of where it enters the Jordan River. Drink from the brook and eat what the ravens bring you. I have commanded them to bring you food."

So Elijah did what the LORD had told him and camped beside Kerith Brook. The ravens brought him bread and meat each morning and evening. He drank from

the brook. But after a while the brook dried up, for there was no rainfall anywhere in the land.

Story based on 1 Kings 16:29-33; 17:1-7 as it appears in the New Living Translation®.

Let's talk about it...

Because of King Ahab's wicked ways, the people suffered greatly. But did you see how God cared for Elijah? This prophet loved and obeyed God, and God cared for him by providing food and water for him. The Bible tells us that God cares for each of us. He knows exactly what we need. Like Elijah, we can trust our Father in Heaven to take care of us.

And if God cares so wonderfully for flowers
that are here today and gone tomorrow,
won't he more surely care for you?
Matthew 6:30, NLT

A Widow's Amazing Faith

How would you describe faith? Faith is believing in something (or someone) when you don't really know what's going to happen. In this story a widow shows her faith when she is asked to give up her last meal.

Discover what she did...

The LORD told Elijah, "Go and live in the village of Zarephath. There is a widow there who will feed you."

When Elijah arrived in Zarephath, he saw a widow gathering sticks, and he asked her for some bread.

But she said, "To tell the truth, I have only a handful of flour left and a little cooking oil in a jug. I was just gathering a few sticks to cook this last meal, and then my son and I will die."

But Elijah said, "Don't be afraid! Cook that 'last meal,' but bake me a little loaf of bread first. For the LORD says: There will always be plenty of flour and oil until the LORD sends rain and the crops grow again!"

So she did as Elijah said, and they all had plenty to eat for many days. For no matter how much they used, there was always enough left in the containers.

Some time later, the woman's son became sick and finally died. She then said to Elijah, "Have you come here to punish my sins by killing my son?"

But Elijah took the boy's body to the upper room and laid the body on his bed. Then Elijah cried out to the LORD, "Why have you brought sadness on this widow who has opened her home to me?"

And he stretched himself out over the child and cried out, "O Lord my God, please let this child's life return to him." The Lord heard Elijah's prayer, and the child came back to life!

Then the woman told Elijah, "Now I know for sure that you are a man of God, and that the Lord truly speaks through you."

Story based on 1 Kings 17:8-24 as it appears in the New Living Translation®.

Let's talk about it...

The widow's faith that God could provide gave her and her son enough food for each day. The widow's son was even brought back to life because of her faith. God wants us to have that kind of faith. When we believe in God and obey him, God tells us that he is able to do the impossible in our lives. Check out the Bible verse below—and believe it!

Even if you had faith as small as a mustard seed you could say to this mountain, "Move from here to there," and it would move. Nothing would be impossible.

Matthew 17:20, NLT

Sitting on the Fence

When someone says, "You're sitting on the fence," it means that you cannot make up your mind. In this story the people of Israel are sitting on the fence about which God to worship and serve.

Check out how God helps them make up their minds...

Ahab went out to meet Elijah. Elijah told him, "You and your family are troublemakers. You have refused to obey the LORD and have worshiped the images of Baal instead. Now bring all the people of Israel to Mount Carmel. Bring the prophets of Baal and of Asherah, who eat at Queen Jezebel's table."

So they went to Mount Carmel, and Elijah said, "If the LORD is God, follow him! But if Baal is God, then follow him!" But the people didn't say a word.

Then Elijah said, "The prophets of Baal may choose a bull and prepare it for sacrifice. I will prepare the other bull and lay it on the altar. Then call on the name of your god, and I will call on the LORD. The god who answers by setting fire to the wood is the true God!"

So the prophets of Baal prepared their bull and placed it on the altar. Then they called on the name of Baal all day, but there was no answer of any kind.

Elijah began to make fun of them. "Maybe your god is away on a trip, or maybe he is asleep!"

Then Elijah prepared the sacrifice. He said, "Fill four large jars with water and pour them over the sacrifice until the water overflows the ditch."

Elijah walked up to the altar and prayed, "O Lord, prove today that you are God and that I am your servant. Answer me so these people will know that you are God and that you are bringing them back to you."

Immediately the fire of the Lord flashed down from Heaven and burned up the sacrifice, the altar, and even the water in the ditch! And when the people saw it, they fell on their faces and cried out, "The Lord is God!"

Story based on 1 Kings 18:16-39 as it appears in the New Living Translation®.

Let's talk about it...

After the "battle of the gods," there were no fence-sitters. Everyone knew who the real God was. People today can learn about God from the Bible, TV, videos, Christian music, etc. As believers, we need to tell everyone about the one true God we believe in and follow. Whom will you tell?

But the Lord is the only true God, the living God. He is the everlasting King!

Jeremiah 10:10, NLT

Elisha's Role Model

Think of someone you really look up to and want to be like someday. Such a person is a role model. For Elisha, the older prophet Elijah was his role model. Elisha wanted to be just like Elijah.

See how God answers Elisha's request...

Elijah and Elisha were traveling. Elijah told Elisha, "Stay here, for the LORD has told me to go to Bethel."

But Elisha answered, "As surely as the LORD lives and you yourself live, I will never leave you!" So they went on together to Bethel.

Then Elijah said to Elisha, "Stay here, for the LORD has told me to go to Jericho."

But Elisha answered the same way again.

Then Elijah said to Elisha, "Stay here, for the LORD has told me to go to the Jordan River."

But again Elisha refused to leave Elijah's side.

Elijah and Elisha stopped beside the Jordan River, and then Elijah folded his coat and struck the water with it. The river divided, and the two of them went across on dry ground!

After they crossed the river, Elijah asked Elisha, "What can I do for you before I am taken away?"

And Elisha answered, "Let me be like you."

Elijah replied, "If you see me when I am taken up, you will get what you ask. But if not, then you won't."

Suddenly a chariot of fire appeared, drawn by horses of fire. It drove between them, and Elijah was carried

by a whirlwind into Heaven. Elisha cried out, "My father! The chariots and horsemen of Israel!"

Then Elisha picked up Elijah's coat and struck the Jordan with it and cried out, "Where is the LORD, the God of Elijah?" Then the river divided, and he crossed.

When the prophets from Jericho saw this, they exclaimed, "Elisha has become just like Elijah!" And they went to meet him and bowed down before him.

Story based on 2 Kings 2:1-15 as it appears in the New Living Translation®.

Let's talk about it...

When Elisha struck the water, he showed that he had faith and wanted to follow God—just like Elijah. It's great to have someone to look up to and try to be like. Whom do you want to be like? Find someone who is a good role model who follows God. Then ask God for help in trying to follow his or her example.

So I ask you to follow my example and do as I do.
I Corinthians 4:16, NLT

More Than Enough

Finish these sentences: "I need more . . . "; "I just gotta . . . " It's easy to think that if you only had more, life would be great. In this story a widow discovers that with God, a little bit is more than enough.
Listen to how God provided for the widow...

One day the widow of one of Elisha's fellow prophets came to Elisha and cried out to him, "My husband who served you is dead, and you know how he obeyed the LORD. But now a money collector has come, threatening to take my two sons as slaves because I have no other way to pay him."

"What can I do to help you?" Elisha asked. "Tell me, what do you have in the house?"

"Nothing at all, except a bottle of olive oil," she answered.

And Elisha said, "Borrow as many empty jars as you can from your friends and neighbors. Then go into your house with your sons and shut the door behind you. Pour olive oil from your bottle into the jars, setting the jars aside as they are filled."

So she did as she was told. Her sons brought many jars to her, and she filled one after another. Soon every container was full to the top!

"Bring me another jar," she said to one of her sons.

"There aren't any more!" he told her. And then the olive oil stopped flowing.

When she told the man of God what had happened, he said to her, "Now sell the olive oil and pay your debts, and there will be enough money left over to support you and your sons."

Story based on 2 Kings 4:1-7 as it appears in the New Living Translation®.

Let's talk about it...

This widow probably never thought she'd be able to pay off her debt with just the little bit of oil she had. But God took the little bit she had and turned it into more than enough. We might think that we can't get by on what God has given us. But God knows what we have and what we need. Whatever God gives us is always enough.

If you will only obey me and let me help you,
then you will have plenty to eat.
Isaiah 1:19, NLT

Never Too Young!

How old do you have to be to do something great for God? Fifteen, twenty, maybe thirty years old? You may be surprised at what you discover in this story...

The king of Aram admired Naaman, the army commander, because through him the LORD had given Aram great victories. But Naaman suffered from leprosy.

One day the maid of Naaman's wife said to her mistress, "My master should go see the prophet in Samaria. He would heal him of leprosy."

The king told Naaman to go visit the prophet. Namaan took many gifts and a letter from his king to give the king of Israel. It said: "I am sending my servant Naaman. I want you to heal him of his leprosy."

When the king of Israel read it, he tore his clothes because he didn't know what to do. But when Elisha, the man of God, heard about the king's reaction, he said: "Why are you so upset? Send Naaman to me."

So Naaman waited at the door of Elisha's house. Elisha sent a messenger out to say, "Go and wash seven times in the Jordan River. Then you will be healed."

But Naaman became angry. He said, "I expected him to wave his hand over the leprosy and call on his God and heal me!" So Naaman turned and went away in a rage.

But his officers talked with him. Finally, Naaman went down to the Jordan River and dipped himself seven times. And he was healed!

Then Naaman and his entire group went back to find Elisha. They stood before him, and Naaman said, "I know at last that there is no God in all the world except in Israel."

Story based on 2 Kings 5:1-15 as it appears in the New Living Translation®.

Let's talk about it...

In this story Naaman is healed and learns about God. But it would not have happened if a young servant girl from Israel hadn't spoken up. We don't know how old the girl was, but she was young *and* a slave. It doesn't matter how old you are or what you are doing. If you are willing to serve God, he can use *you* to do some great things for him.

Don't let anyone think less of you because you are young. Be an example to all believers in what you teach, in the way you live, in your love, your faith, and your purity.

1 Timothy 4:12, NLT

If no one is watching, do you still have to obey your parents, your teachers, or even God? Jonah discovered the hard way that obeying God is always the best choice—no matter who's looking!

Learn from Jonah's mistake...

The LORD gave this message to Jonah: "Go to the great city of Nineveh! Announce my judgment against it because I have seen how wicked its people are."

But Jonah got up and tried to get away from the LORD. He went down to the seacoast and got on a ship.

But as the ship was sailing along, the LORD caused a violent storm that could sink the ship. Fearing for their lives, the sailors shouted to their gods for help. And all this time Jonah was asleep. So the captain went down and shouted, "How can you sleep? Get up and pray to your god! Maybe he will spare our lives."

So Jonah told them, "I worship the LORD, the God of Heaven, who made the sea and the land." Then he told them that he was running away from the LORD.

"Throw me into the sea," Jonah said, "and it will become calm again. This terrible storm is all my fault."

Then the sailors picked Jonah up and threw him into the raging sea, and the storm stopped at once! The sailors were amazed by the LORD's great power, and they offered him a sacrifice and promised to serve him.

Now the LORD had planned for a great fish to swallow Jonah. And he was in the fish for three days.

Then Jonah prayed to the LORD: "I called to you from the world of the dead, and you heard me! When I lost all hope, I turned my thoughts once more to the LORD. My salvation comes from the LORD alone."

Then the LORD ordered the fish to spit up Jonah on the beach. And the LORD spoke to Jonah again: "Go to Nineveh and deliver the message of judgment."

This time Jonah obeyed the LORD's command.

Story based on Jonah 1:1–3:3 as it appears in the New Living Translation®.

Let's talk about it...

Jonah thought if he ran fast enough and far enough he wouldn't have to obey God. But God knows everything— what we're thinking, what we say, what we do, and where we are. Sometimes we want to run from what God wants us to do. That's when we need to remember Jonah— and obey God from the start.

Young people who obey the law are wise.
Proverbs 28:7, NLT

Worship While You Work

When you have lots of chores, do you moan, groan, and think of how to get out of them? Or do you get right to work? God's people had a *huge* job facing them. Read how they responded...

In his very first month as king, Hezekiah reopened the doors of the Temple of the LORD, and repaired them. He called the priests and Levites and said, "Purify yourselves, and purify the Temple. Our ancestors turned their backs on the LORD. That is why the LORD's anger has come to Judah and Jerusalem. I will make an agreement with the LORD so that his fierce anger will turn away from us. You must get busy and do what God wants!"

Then the Levites got right to work. They purified themselves and began to purify the Temple. They were careful to follow all the LORD's instructions.

Then the Levites went to King Hezekiah and told him: "We have purified the Temple. We have also put back all the utensils taken by King Ahaz when he closed the Temple. They are now in front of the altar of the LORD, purified and ready for use."

Early the next morning King Hezekiah gathered the city officials and went to the Temple of the LORD. Everyone worshiped the LORD until all the burnt offerings were finished. Then the king and everyone with him praised God with joy and bowed in worship.

Then Hezekiah said, "The special service has come to an end. Now bring your sacrifices and thanksgiving

offerings to the Temple." So the Temple services would be able to continue. And all the people rejoiced greatly because of what God had done for the people, for everything had happened so quickly.

Story based on 2 Chronicles 29:3-36 as it appears in the New Living Translation®.

Let's talk about it...

It took a lot of work to clean up the Temple. But King Hezekiah, the priests, Levites, and the people wanted to obey God's instructions. They were excited and really enjoyed doing the work. When we do what God wants, it's like God is our work partner. Doing what God wants us to do with a good attitude is a great way to praise him.

Never be lazy in your work,
but serve the Lord enthusiastically.
Romans 12:11, NLT

A Time to Confess

Imagine discovering that you've done something wrong. Would you say you're sorry, or would you make excuses? In this story King Josiah discovers that Israel has not been following God's law.

See what Josiah does...

Josiah was eight years old when he became king. He did what was pleasing in the LORD's sight and followed the example of his ancestor David. When Josiah was twenty-six, he sent Shaphan to the Temple of the LORD, saying, "Go to Hilkiah the high priest and have him count this money. Give this money to the men in charge the Temple's repairs, so they can pay workers to repair the Temple."

Hilkiah the high priest said to Shaphan, "I found the Book of the Law in the LORD's Temple!"

Shaphan returned to the king and told King Josiah what Hilkiah had found. When the king heard the Book of the Law read, he tore his clothes in despair. Then he ordered: "Go to the Temple and speak to the LORD. Ask him about the words written in this scroll. The LORD is angry because our ancestors have not obeyed the Book of the Law."

So Hilkiah the priest, Shaphan, and the others went to talk with the prophet Huldah. She said to them, "Tell the king of Judah: 'This is what the LORD, the God of Israel, says: You cried to me in sadness when you heard that I said this city and its people would be destroyed. I will not send this punishment until you have died

and been buried in peace.'" So they took her message back to the king.

Then the king read to the people of Judah the Book of the Covenant that had been found in the LORD's Temple. The king agreed with everything written in the scroll, and all the people agreed to obey what was written there.

Story based on 2 Kings 22:1–23:3 as it appears in the New Living Translation®.

Let's talk about it...

As soon as King Josiah knew that he was guilty, he did the right thing by telling God he was sorry. Saying that we didn't know we were sinning, or that somebody made us do it, is not an excuse for disobeying God. When we admit when we are wrong and are sorry for what we have done, God forgives us.

But if we confess our sins to him, he is faithful and just to forgive us and to cleanse us from every wrong.
1 John 1:9, NLT

Daniel's Veggie Diet

Think of something you gave up in order to obey God. Maybe it was skipping a sleepover on a Saturday. Or not joining a team that plays on Sunday. Sometimes God's followers have to do that.

Find out what Daniel and his friends give up to obey God. . .

King Nebuchadnezzar of Babylon attacked Jerusalem. The Lord gave him victory over Judah. Then the king gave this order: "Choose strong, healthy, and good-looking young male prisoners," he said. "Make sure they are filled with knowledge and good sense. Help them learn our language and teachings."

Daniel and three of his friends were four of the young men chosen. The king gave them the best food and wine from his own kitchens. But Daniel made up his mind not to eat the king's food and wine because it would not please God. So Daniel asked the chief official for permission to eat other things. Now God had given the chief official great respect for Daniel. But he was worried about Daniel's suggestion.

Daniel talked it over with the attendant, saying, "Test us for ten days on a diet of vegetables and water. After ten days, see how we look compared to the others. Then decide if we can continue eating our diet." So the attendant agreed.

At the end of the ten days, Daniel and his friends looked healthier than all the other young men. So after

that, the attendant fed them only vegetables. God gave these four young men an unusual ability to learn the writings and science of the time. And God gave Daniel an understanding of the meanings of dreams.

Daniel and his friends were added to the king's regular staff of advisers. When the king had important questions, the king found the advice of Daniel and his friends to be ten times better than that of all the magicians and enchanters in his entire kingdom.

Story based on Daniel 1:1-20 as it appears in the New Living Translation®.

Let's talk about it...

Daniel and his friends gave up Nebuchadnezzar's palace food to obey God. But God gave them something better. They became healthier and wiser than everyone else. Sometimes we give up something to obey God. But what he gives back to us is always better than what we gave up.

You have given me greater joy than those
who have abundant harvests of grain and wine.

Psalm 4:7, NLT

Bow or Burn?

Here's your choice—follow a rule that you know is wrong or obey God. What would you do? Daniel's three friends have to make this decision. They know if they don't obey the rule, they will die.

Check out what they decide...

King Nebuchadnezzar made a gold statue ninety feet tall and nine feet wide. He told all his officials to come to the statue. When everyone arrived, a man shouted out, "When you hear the music, bow to the ground to worship the statue. Anyone who refuses will be thrown into a furnace."

But some astrologers said to King Nebuchadnezzar, "There are some Jews—Shadrach, Meshach, and Abednego—who refuse to worship the gold statue."

Then the king was very, very angry and told them, "Bow down and worship the statue or you will be thrown into the blazing furnace."

They answered, "If we are thrown into the blazing furnace, the God we serve is able to save us. We will never serve your gods or worship the gold statue."

Nebuchadnezzar was so angry that he commanded the furnace be heated seven times hotter than usual. Then some soldiers tied up the three young men and threw them into the blazing furnace. The furnace was so hot that it killed the soldiers as they threw the three men in!

But suddenly, Nebuchadnezzar jumped up and exclaimed, "I see four men, untied, walking around.

They aren't even hurt by the flames! And the fourth looks like a heavenly being!"

Then Nebuchadnezzar shouted for them to come out of the fire. Not a hair on their heads was singed!

Then Nebuchadnezzar said, "Praise to the God of Shadrach, Meshach, and Abednego! He sent his angel to rescue his servants who trusted in him. There is no other god who can rescue like this!"

Story based on Daniel 3:1-29 as it appears in the New Living Translation®.

Let's talk about it...

Shadrach, Meshach, and Abednego loved God and weren't afraid of Nebuchadnezzar and his fiery furnace. They knew it was better to die than to turn from God. We may not have to die to obey God. But we may be teased about going to church or carrying a Bible. We need to remember that God deserves to be put first.

You must love the Lord your God with all your heart, all your soul, and all your mind.

Matthew 22:37, NLT

A Powerful Message

Sometimes we don't pay attention to messages because of how we feel about the person who delivers them. In this story God really got King Belshazzar's attention with a powerful message.

Uncover why it was such a powerful message...

King Belshazzar gave a great feast for his nobles. They honored their idols with the gold and silver cups stolen from the Temple of God.

At that very moment they saw the fingers of a human hand writing on the wall of the palace. The king was so terrified that his knees knocked together.

The king told the enchanters, astrologers, and fortune-tellers, "Whoever can tell me what this means will be honored highly!" But no one could read it.

Then the queen mother said, "Daniel is a man filled with special knowledge and understanding. He will tell you what this means."

So Daniel was brought before the king. The king promised him purple robes of royal honor, a gold chain, and that he would become the third highest ruler, if he would tell them the meaning of the words.

Daniel answered the king, "Keep your gifts, but I will tell you what the writing means. God gave glory and honor to Nebuchadnezzar. But when his heart and mind were full of pride, God took his glory away.

"You knew this, Belshazzar, yet you insulted the Lord by drinking wine in cups from his Temple while praising false gods. So God has sent this message:

'Mene, mene, tekel, parsin.' It means: God has brought your rule to an end. You have failed the test, and your kingdom has been divided and given away."

That very night the Babylonian king was killed. And Darius the Mede took over the kingdom.

Story based on Daniel 5:1-31 as it appears in the New Living Translation®.

Let's talk about it...

The writing on the wall was a reminder to Belshazzar of God's power. For those who disobey God, his power is something to be feared. When we love and honor God by what we say and do, we don't have to be afraid of God's power. We know his power will be used to help and protect us in all we do.

You are the God of miracles and wonders! You demonstrate your awesome power among the nations.
Psalm 77:14, NLT

Daniel in the Lions' Den

We all have habits. Some habits, like biting our nails, are bad. Other habits, like brushing our teeth, keep us healthy. Daniel has a great habit of praying to God— and nothing is going to stop him.

Discover what Daniel's habit got him...

Because of Daniel's great ability, the king planned to place him in charge of the whole empire. The other officials began looking for something bad about Daniel.

So the officials went to the king and said, "We think that you should make a law that anyone who prays to anyone except you will be thrown to the lions. Sign this law so it cannot be changed."

When Daniel learned that the law had been signed, he prayed, just as he had always done. The officials found Daniel praying. Then they told the king, "That man Daniel from Judah still prays to his God."

Hearing this, the king was very angry with himself for signing the law. He spent the rest of the day looking for a way to save Daniel. But the officials said, "You cannot change a law you have signed."

So at last the king gave orders for Daniel to be thrown into the den of lions. The king said to him, "May your God, whom you worship, rescue you."

Early the next day, the king hurried out to the lions' den. He called out, "Daniel, did your God rescue you?"

Daniel answered, "Long live the king! My God sent his angel to shut the lions' mouths."

The king was overjoyed and ordered that Daniel be lifted from the den. Not a scratch was found on him because he had trusted in his God. Then the king gave orders for the officials to be thrown to the lions.

Then King Darius sent this message to the people of every nation: "Everyone should respect the God of Daniel. He saves his people; he performs wonderful miracles in the heavens and on Earth."

Story based on Daniel 6:3-27 as it appears in the New Living Translation®.

Let's talk about it...

Even though Daniel faced death, prayer was such a part of his life that he could not—and would not—stop praying. Daniel knew that prayer was a very special way to talk to God. God is always ready to hear us pray and answer our prayers. Prayer time is a wonderful time to visit with God each day.

Devote yourselves to prayer with an alert mind and a thankful heart.

Colossians 4:2, NLT

Queen for a Time Like This

You and your friends probably like a lot of the same things. That's why you hang out together. But what makes each of you special are the things you do well that God has given only to you.

Find out about Queen Esther's special gift...

There was a Jewish man named Mordecai, who had a beautiful young cousin named Esther. When her parents died, Mordecai adopted her. Esther was one of the women brought to King Xerxes when he was looking for a new queen. The king liked Esther so much that he made her queen. Esther told no one she was a Jew, for Mordecai had told her not to tell.

Some time later, Xerxes made Haman the most powerful official in the empire next to himself. Everyone bowed before Haman, but Mordecai refused to bow down. Haman was so angry that he decided to destroy all the Jews because Mordecai was a Jew.

Mordecai told Esther to go to the king to beg for her people. He said, "If you keep quiet now, rescue for the Jews will arise from some other place, but you and your relatives will die. Maybe you have become queen for just such a time as this."

So Esther went to the king. When he saw Esther, he welcomed her. Then Esther invited the king and Haman to a banquet.

At the banquet the king said, "Tell me what you want, Queen Esther. I will give it to you, even if it is half the kingdom!"

And so Esther answered, "My wish is that my life and the lives of my people will be spared."

When King Xerxes demanded to know what was going on, Esther replied, "This wicked Haman is our enemy." Haman grew pale with fright. "Hang Haman!" the king ordered.

Esther had done well. The Jews rejoiced and had a great celebration.

Story based on Esther 1:1-8:17 as it appears in the New Living Translation®.

Let's talk about it...

God gave Esther the gift of beauty. But God also gave Esther a job to do because of her special position as queen. Think about the gifts God has given you. Are you really good at math? Do you play piano well? Do you make friends easily? Look for ways to use your special gifts to serve God and help others.

God has given each of us the ability
to do certain things well.
Romans 12:6, NLT

A Living Example

One of the best ways to learn something new is to watch someone show you how to do it. Ezra knew that was a good way to teach others about how to live for God.

Discover how Ezra's life was a great example for others...

Ezra was a priest who knew the teachings of the law of Moses. Ezra had decided to study and obey the law of the LORD and to teach those laws to the people of Israel.

King Artaxerxes gave the following letter to Ezra: "Greetings from Artaxerxes, the king of kings, to Ezra the priest.

"Any of the people of Israel in my kingdom may return to Jerusalem with you. Check out the situation in Judah and Jerusalem, based on your God's law, which is in your hand.

"I, Artaxerxes the king, hereby send this order. All the treasurers in the area west of the Euphrates River will give you whatever you ask. I also order that no worker in this Temple of God will have to pay taxes of any kind.

"And you, Ezra, are to use the wisdom God has given you to choose leaders who know your God's laws. These men will rule the people. If the people don't know those laws, you must teach them. Anyone who refuses to obey the law of your God and the law of the king will be punished immediately."

So Ezra came to Jerusalem from Babylon, and King Artaxerxes gave him everything he asked for because the LORD was helping Ezra. Some of the leaders of Israel traveled to Jerusalem with Ezra to make the Temple of the LORD beautiful and worship God there.

Story based on Ezra 7:6-28 as it appears in the New Living Translation®.

Let's talk about it...

Why did God choose Ezra for this job? It was because Ezra studied and obeyed God's Word. But Ezra didn't teach just by what he said. Ezra also taught by how he acted. We can follow Ezra's example. First, we need to know what the Bible teaches. Then we need to follow what it says. Our words and our actions will help others know about God.

How can a young person stay pure? By obeying your word and following its rules.

Psalm 119:9, NLT

Doing Your Part for God

Next time you go to the movies, stay for the credits, the list of names at the end of the movie. You will see how many people it took to make just one movie. This story includes a credit list of the people who helped get one huge job done.

Learn why we need to work together...

Before Nehemiah moved back to Israel, he was the wine taster for the king of Persia. Although that was an important job, God had a different job in mind for Nehemiah. God wanted Nehemiah to lead the rebuilding of the temple in Jerusalem, where Ezra was living. The city wall needed to be rebuilt so the people would feel safe. This project could be finished only if all of the people of Israel worked together.

So Nehemiah went out to see the broken wall and burned gates of the city. Then he told the priests and leaders, "The wall of our city lies in ruins, and its gates are burned. Let us rebuild the wall of Jerusalem and free ourselves of this shame."

The leaders answered, "Good! Let's rebuild the wall!" So they began the good work.

Priests, people from the city of Jericho, people from Tekoa, the leaders of Jerusalem, people from Zanoah, goldsmiths, merchants, temple servants, sons, and daughters all worked together to repair the wall.

After just fifty-two days, the wall was finished. When their enemies and the surrounding nations

heard about it, they were afraid and lost their self-confidence. They understood this work had been done with the help of the LORD God.

Story based on Nehemiah 2–3; 6:15, 16 as it appears in the New Living Translation®.

Let's talk about it...

Everybody had a job to do—and they did it. The result? The walls around the city of Jerusalem were rebuilt in a record-breaking fifty-two days. The work of God's church is like that. When everyone works together, great things can be done. How can you contribute to helping God's work get done at church, at school, or at home?

There are different kinds of service in the church, but it is the same Lord we are serving.

1 Corinthians 12:5, NLT

Believe It—Or Not?

When your friend tells you an amazing story, do you believe it or not? That might depend on whether your friend usually tells the truth. In this story Zechariah heard some pretty amazing news.
See if he believed it or not...

It all begins with a Jewish priest, Zechariah, who lived when Herod was king of Judea. Zechariah and his wife, Elizabeth, pleased God, because they were careful to obey all of his commandments. They had no children, and they were both very old.

One day Zechariah was in the Temple burning incense in the Lord's presence. An angel of the Lord appeared. Zechariah was full of fear. But the angel said, "Don't be afraid, Zechariah! God has heard your prayer, and your wife, Elizabeth, will have a son! You are to name him John. You will have great joy, and many will be happy with you at his birth, for he will be great in the eyes of the Lord. He will go before the Lord's coming, preparing the people for his arrival."

Zechariah said to the angel, "How can I know this will happen? My wife and I are very old."

Then the angel said, "God sent me to bring you this good news! Now, since you didn't believe me, you won't be able to speak until the child is born."

When Elizabeth heard the news of the baby, she exclaimed, "How kind the Lord is!"

Now it was time for Elizabeth's baby to be born, and it was a boy. The relatives and friends wanted to

name the baby Zechariah, after his father. But Elizabeth said, "No! His name is John!"

"There is no one in all your family by that name," they exclaimed. So they asked Zechariah for the baby's name, and he wrote, "John!" Instantly Zechariah could speak again, and he began praising God.

Story based on Luke 1:5-25, 57-64 as it appears in the New Living Translation®.

Let's talk about it...

Even though God's angel brought the message, Zechariah had a hard time believing the news. But God's promises are always true even when they seem impossible. Throughout the Bible, God kept his promises to his people. Not one promise failed. God still keeps his promises to us. Believe it! Whatever God promises will surely happen.

Every promise of the LORD your God has come true.
Not a single one has failed!
Joshua 23:14, NLT

A Birth Fit for a King?

What kind of crib should a baby prince have? Should it be made of gold or of old, dirty wood? Should it be decorated with jewels or with animal feed?
Check out the unusual details of the birth of this king...

At that time the Roman emperor, Augustus, ordered that a list should be made of people who lived in the Roman Empire. Joseph, a descendant of King David, had to go to Bethlehem in Judea to sign for this census. He took Mary with him. It was almost time for her to have a baby.

And while they were in Bethlehem, Mary gave birth to her first child, a son. She wrapped him snugly in strips of cloth and laid him in a manger, because there was no room for them in the village inn.

That night some shepherds were in the fields, guarding their flocks of sheep. Suddenly, an angel of the Lord appeared among them. The shepherds were terribly frightened, but the angel calmed them. "Don't be afraid!" he said. "I bring you good news of great joy for everyone! The Savior has been born tonight in Bethlehem! You will find a baby lying in a manger, wrapped snugly in strips of cloth!"

Suddenly, the angel was joined by many more angels who were praising God saying: "Glory to God in the highest Heaven, and peace on Earth to all who please God."

When the angels left, the shepherds said to each other, "Let's go see this wonderful thing that has happened."

They ran to the village and found Mary and Joseph. They saw the baby lying in the manger. Then the shepherds told everyone what had happened and what the angel had said to them about this child. Everyone who heard the story was amazed at what had happened.

Story based on Luke 2:1-20 as it appears in the New Living Translation®.

Let's talk about it...

Jesus is the King of kings. But his birth wasn't very royal, was it? Jesus' crib was an animal's feeding trough. And the first people to greet Jesus were poor, smelly shepherds. All these details show us that Jesus is a different kind of king. Jesus was born as a baby and grew up just like us— but without any sin. Jesus lived on Earth so he could die for our sins. Jesus did not come to just be king of the world, but king of our hearts as well.

Look, your king is coming to you. He is righteous and victorious, yet he is humble.

Zechariah 9:9, NLT

What Are You Waiting For?

How long would you wait for something you *really* want? Would you wait a week or a month? How about a year? The people in our story were willing to wait for something they wanted very much.
Decide if it was worth it...

Eight days later the baby was named Jesus, the name given him by the angel before he was born.

Then his parents took him to Jerusalem to present him to the Lord.

Now there was a man named Simeon who lived in Jerusalem. The Holy Spirit let Simeon know that he would not die until he had seen the Lord's Messiah. That day the Spirit led him to the Temple. So when Mary and Joseph came to present baby Jesus to the Lord as the law said, Simeon was there. He took the child in his arms and praised God, saying, "Lord, now I can die in peace! As you promised me, I have seen the Savior you have given to all people. He is a light to show God to the nations, and he is the glory of your people Israel!"

Then Simeon blessed Joseph and Mary, saying, "Many in Israel will turn against this child. But he will be the greatest joy to many others."

Anna, a prophet, was also there in the Temple. She came along just as Simeon was talking with Mary and Joseph. She began praising God, too. She talked about Jesus to everyone who had been waiting for the promised king to come and free Jerusalem.

Jesus' parents finished doing everything required in the law of the Lord. Then they returned home to Nazareth in Galilee. There Jesus grew up healthy and strong. He was filled with wisdom beyond his years, and he pleased God.

Story based on Luke 2:21-52 as it appears in the New Living Translation®.

Let's talk about it...

Anna and Simeon had grown old waiting to see Jesus. But their faith in God's promise of a Savior helped them as they waited. We may want something very much. We may pray for God to make it happen. But sometimes God makes us wait until the time is just right. That's when we need to ask God for patience and faith like Simeon's and Anna's.

Be still in the presence of the LORD, and wait patiently for him to act.

Psalm 37:7, NLT

A Wise Way to Worship

You probably don't travel very far to attend worship. If you had to travel more than one hundred miles, you'd probably find a new church! The men in this story traveled *thousands* of miles to find Jesus. Find out what they did when they arrived...

Jesus was born in the town of Bethlehem in Judea. About that time some wise men from eastern lands arrived in Jerusalem, asking, "Where is the newborn king of the Jews? We have seen his star as it arose, and we have come to worship him."

King Herod was upset by their question. He called a meeting of the leading priests and teachers of religious law, and asked, "Where did the prophets say the Messiah would be born?"

"In Bethlehem," they said. "The prophet wrote: 'O Bethlehem of Judah, you are not just a lowly village in Judah, for a ruler will come from you who will be the shepherd for my people Israel.'"

Then Herod asked the wise men to come see him. At this meeting he learned the time when they first saw the star. Then he told them, "Go to Bethlehem and search carefully for the child. And when you find him, come back and tell me so that I can go and worship him, too!"

After talking with the king, the wise men went on their way. The star went ahead of them and stopped over the place where little Jesus was. The wise men entered the house where little Jesus and his mother, Mary, were, and they fell down before him and worshiped him.

Then they opened their treasure chests and gave him gifts of gold, frankincense, and myrrh. But when it was time to leave, they went home another way, because God had warned them in a dream not go back to Herod.

Story based on Matthew 2:1-12 as it appears in the New Living Translation®.

Let's talk about it...

These wise men went to a lot of trouble to find Jesus. When the wise men found Jesus, they were filled with joy. The wise men worshiped Jesus and gave him gifts. What a great example for us! We can be like the wise men when we worship Jesus. We can be filled with joy as we sing and praise Jesus and give him gifts of our time, money, and talents.

Come, let us worship and bow down.
Let us kneel before the LORD our maker.
Psalm 95:6, NLT

A Change in Plans

Have you and your friends ever made plans, only to be told by your parents, "I don't think so." King Herod made some plans—to kill the newborn king— to protect his power.

But God had another plan...

After the wise men were gone, an angel of the Lord came to Joseph in a dream. "Get up and hurry to Egypt with the child and his mother," the angel said. "Stay there until I tell you to return, because King Herod is going to try to kill the child." That night Joseph left for Egypt with Jesus and Mary.

Herod was very angry when he learned that the wise men had tricked him. He sent soldiers to kill all the boys in and around Bethlehem who were two years old and under. He did that because the wise men had told him the star first appeared to them about two years earlier. Herod's cruel action made the words of Jeremiah come true:

"A painful cry is heard in Ramah. Mothers are crying for their children because their children are dead."

Later when Herod died, an angel of the Lord came in a dream to Joseph in Egypt and told him, "Get up and take Jesus and his mother back to the land of Israel. Those who were trying to kill the child are dead." So Joseph returned immediately to Israel with Jesus and his mother. But when Joseph learned that the new ruler was Herod's son Archelaus, he was afraid. Then, in

another dream, Joseph was warned to go to Galilee. So
they went and lived in a town called Nazareth. When
that happened, the words of another prophet came true.

Story based on Matthew 2:13-23 as it appears in the New Living Translation®.

Let's talk about it...

Herod's big mistake was believing he was in charge. And
Herod was going to do all he could to stay in power.
But as we read this story and see how God protected
Mary, Joseph, and their tiny son, we see who's really in
charge. If we love and obey God, then we can become
partners in carrying out his plans. How exciting!

May your will be done here on earth,
just as it is in heaven.
Matthew 6:10, NLT

Jesus and His Parents

Think of a time when it was hard for you to obey your parents. If obeying your parents is hard for you, imagine how Jesus felt. Mary and Joseph were his parents, but he was *their* God.

See what Jesus did when his parents were upset with him...

Every year Jesus' parents went to Jerusalem for the Passover festival. When Jesus was twelve years old, they attended the festival as usual. After the celebration was over, they started home to Nazareth, but Jesus stayed behind in Jerusalem. His parents didn't miss him at first. They thought he was with friends among the other travelers. But when he didn't show up that evening, they started to look for him among their relatives and friends.

When Mary and Joseph couldn't find Jesus, they went back to Jerusalem to search for him there. Three days later they finally discovered him. He was in the Temple, sitting among the religious teachers, discussing questions with them. And all who heard Jesus were amazed at his understanding and his answers.

His parents didn't know what to think. His mother said to him, "Why have you done this to us? Your father and I have been searching for you everywhere."

"But why did you need to search?" he asked. "You should have known that I would be in my Father's house." But they didn't understand what he meant.

Then Jesus returned to Nazareth with his parents and was obedient to them. So Jesus grew both in height and in wisdom, and he was loved by God and by all who knew him.

Story based on Luke 2:41-52 as it appears in the New Living Translation®.

Let's talk about it...

Even though Jesus was God, he respected his parents by returning to Nazareth and obeying them. Jesus showed us how to be obedient to our parents and to do what they ask without complaining. When we obey and respect our parents, we are following Jesus' example. And guess what? We're pleasing our heavenly Father, too.

Honor your father and mother,
as the LORD your God commanded you.
Deuteronomy 5:16, NLT

The Coming Attraction

When you go to the movies, you usually have to sit through the "coming attractions." These previews tell you what you can expect to see. In a way, John the Baptist acted as a preview to Jesus—the main attraction!

Look at this preview...

In the book of the prophet Isaiah, God said, "Look, I am sending my messenger ahead of you, and he will prepare your way. He is a voice shouting in the wilderness: 'Prepare a pathway for the Lord's coming! Make a straight road for him!'"

This messenger was John the Baptist. He lived in the wilderness and his clothes were woven from camel hair. John wore a leather belt; he ate locusts and wild honey. John was preaching that people should be baptized. This would show that they had turned from their sins and turned to God to be forgiven. People from Jerusalem and from all over Judea traveled out into the wilderness to see and hear John. And when they told about their sins, he baptized them in the Jordan River. John the Baptist announced: "Someone is coming soon who is far greater than I am—so much greater that I am not even worthy to be his slave. I baptize you with water, but he will baptize you with the Holy Spirit!"

One day Jesus came from Nazareth in Galilee, and he was baptized by John in the Jordan River. When Jesus came up out of the water, he saw the heavens split open. Then the Holy Spirit came down like a dove

on him. A voice came from Heaven saying, "You are my beloved Son, and I am very pleased with you."

Story based on Mark 1:2-11 as it appears in the New Living Translation®.

Let's talk about it...

John was the messenger who was to prepare people for the coming of Jesus. It was John's job to make sure that everyone knew who Jesus was so they would listen to him. If we know Jesus, we can be like John the Baptist. We can tell other people about who Jesus is and what he has done for us. Help others discover the main attraction.

And you must also tell others about me because you have been with me from the beginning.

John 15:27, NLT

The Temptation Fighter

Sometimes it's hard to walk away from something we *really* want—even if we know it's wrong. Maybe you've been tempted to sneak an extra cookie or cheat on a test. Jesus was tempted too.

Read how Jesus resisted Satan's temptations...

After Jesus was baptized and filled with the Holy Spirit, he left the Jordan River. Jesus was led by the Spirit to go out into the wilderness. There the Devil tempted him for forty days. He ate nothing all that time and was very hungry.

Then the Devil said to him, "If you are the Son of God, change this stone into a loaf of bread."

But Jesus told him, "No! The Scriptures say: 'People need more than bread for their life.'"

Then the Devil took him up and showed him all the kingdoms of the world in a moment of time. The Devil told him, "I will give you the glory of these kingdoms and power over them—because they are mine to give to anyone I please. I will give it all to you if you will bow down and worship me."

Jesus answered, "The Scriptures say, 'You must worship the Lord your God; serve only him.'"

Then the Devil took him to Jerusalem, to the highest point of the Temple, and said, "If you are the Son of God, jump off! For the Scriptures say, 'God orders his angels to protect and guard you. And they will hold you with their hands to keep you from hitting your foot on a stone.'"

Jesus answered, "The Scriptures also say: 'Do not test the Lord your God.'"

When the Devil had finished tempting Jesus, he left him until the next chance came.

Story based on Luke 4:1-13 as it appears in the New Living Translation®.

Let's talk about it...

Did you see how Jesus fought off Satan's temptations? He used God's Word. We can do the same. When we are tempted to do something wrong, we can go to the Bible for help. We also can ask Jesus for help. Jesus knows what we're feeling. He's been tempted in the same way, so he can help us beat any temptation.

Since he himself has gone through suffering and temptation, he is able to help us when we are being tempted.

Hebrews 2:18, NLT

Peter Meets Jesus

If you have ever met someone famous, you may have felt uncomfortable, even shy, around that person. After all, that person is famous, and you're not. In this story Simon Peter came face-to-face with Jesus. Check out Simon's reaction...

One day as Jesus was preaching on the shore of the Sea of Galilee, great crowds pressed in on him to listen to the Word of God. He noticed two empty boats at the water's edge, for the fishermen had left them and were washing their nets. Stepping into one of the boats, Jesus asked Simon Peter, the boat's owner, to push it out into the water. So Jesus sat in the boat and taught the crowds from the sea.

When he had finished speaking, he said to Simon, "Now go out where it is deeper and let down your nets, and you will catch many fish."

"Master," Simon Peter replied, "we worked hard all last night and didn't catch a thing. But if you say so, we'll try again." And this time their nets were so full they began to tear! A shout for help brought their partners in the other boat. Soon both boats were filled with fish and about to sink.

When Simon Peter understood what had happened, he fell to his knees before Jesus and said, "Oh, Lord, please leave me—I'm too much of a sinner to be around you." For he was surprised by the size of their catch, as were the others with him. His partners, James and John, the sons of Zebedee, were also amazed.

Jesus replied to Simon, "Don't be afraid! From now on you'll be fishing for people!" And as soon as they landed, they left everything and followed Jesus.

Story based on Luke 5:1-11 as it appears in the New Living Translation®.

Let's talk about it...

When Peter met Jesus, his life changed forever. Peter realized how holy Jesus was—and how sinful Peter was compared to Jesus. But Jesus still wanted Peter to be his follower. That's good news for us. We don't have to be perfect to follow Jesus. We just have to believe in Jesus as our Savior and be willing to join him. Are you willing?

We are made right in God's sight when we trust in Jesus Christ to take away our sins.

Romans 3:22, NLT

The Life of the Party

A party without good food and drinks will get boring pretty fast. The wedding celebration in this story started to fizzle when the wine ran out. People would think badly of the bride's father for not having enough for his guests. Discover how Jesus helped him out...

Jesus' mother was a guest at a wedding celebration in the village of Cana in Galilee. Jesus and his disciples were also invited to the celebration. The wine supply ran out during the party, so Jesus' mother spoke to him about the problem. "They have no more wine," she told him.

"Why are you telling me?" Jesus asked.

But his mother told the servants, "Do whatever he tells you."

Six stone waterpots were standing there; they were used for Jewish ceremonial purposes. The pots each held twenty to thirty gallons of water. Jesus told the servants, "Fill the jars with water." When the jars had been filled to the top, he said, "Dip some out and take it to the bride's father." So they followed Jesus' instructions.

When the bride's father tasted the water that was now wine, he called the bridegroom over. "Usually a host serves the best wine first," he said. "Then, when everyone is full and doesn't care, he brings out the less expensive wines. But you have kept the best until now!"

This miracle at Cana in Galilee was Jesus' first display of his glory. And his disciples believed in him.

Story based on John 2:1-11 as it appears in the New Living Translation®.

Let's talk about it...

It would have been embarrassing for a Jewish family to run out of wine at a wedding. But Jesus helped this family with a miracle. He turned six large pots of water into the very best wine! We can trust Jesus to give what's best for us, too. He gives us food, clothes, and everything else we need to live. Jesus also gives us joy, love, and faith to follow him.

My purpose is to give life in all its fullness.
John 10:10, NLT

Getting to Know God

If you want to get to know a person, you spend time with that person, ask questions, and talk. But how do you get to know God—*really* get to know him? What does it take?

Jesus had an interesting answer for one religious leader...

After dark one evening, a Jewish religious leader named Nicodemus (a Pharisee) came to speak with Jesus. "Teacher," he said, "we all know that God has sent you to teach us. Your miracles are proof enough that God is with you."

Jesus answered, "The truth is, no one can enter the Kingdom of God without being born of water and the Spirit. Human life can only give human life, but the Holy Spirit gives new life from Heaven."

"What do you mean?" Nicodemus asked.

Jesus said, "God so loved the world that he gave his only Son, so that everyone who believes in him will not die but have eternal life. God did not send his Son into the world to judge it, but to save the world.

"There is no judgment waiting for those who trust him. But those who do not trust him have already been judged for not believing in the only Son of God. Their judgment is based on this fact: The light from Heaven came into the world, but they loved the darkness more than the light, for their actions were evil. They hate the light because they want to sin in

the darkness. They stay away from the light for fear their sins will be seen and they will be punished. But those who do what is right come to the light gladly, so everyone can see that they are doing what God wants."

Story based on John 3:1-21 as it appears in the New Living Translation®.

Let's talk about it...

Religious leaders were supposed to know a lot about God. But Nicodemus didn't understand what Jesus was talking about. What Nicodemus needed was the Holy Spirit to help him really *know* God. We can know a lot *about* God. But we won't *really* know God personally until the Holy Spirit gives us new life and understanding.

But I will send you the Counselor—the Spirit of truth. He will come to you from the Father and will tell you all about me.

John 15:26, NLT

Got to See Jesus!

How far would you go to make sure your friends knew about Jesus? Would you invite them to church? Take them to a Christian rock concert? Buy them a Bible? Learn how far these four friends were willing to go...

Jesus returned to Capernaum. The news of his arrival spread quickly through the town. Soon the house where he was staying was so packed with visitors that there wasn't room for one more person, not even outside the door. As Jesus was teaching them, four men arrived carrying a paralyzed man on a mat. They couldn't get to Jesus through the crowd, so they dug through the clay roof of the house. Then they lowered the sick man on his mat, right down in front of Jesus. Seeing their faith, Jesus said to the paralyzed man, "My son, your sins are forgiven."

But some of the teachers of religious law who were sitting there said to themselves, "What? This is against God! Only God can forgive sins!"

Jesus knew what they were talking about, so he said to them, "Why do you think this is against God? Is it easier to say to the paralyzed man, 'Your sins are forgiven' or 'Get up, pick up your mat, and walk'? I will prove that I, the Son of Man, have the power on Earth to forgive sins." Then Jesus turned to the paralyzed man and said, "Stand up, take your mat, and go on home, because you are healed!"

The man jumped up, took the mat, and pushed his way through the surprised crowd. Then everyone praised God, exclaiming, "We've never seen anything like this before!"

Story based on Mark 2:1-12 as it appears in the New Living Translation®.

Let's talk about it...

Did you see what these four friends did? They didn't let any problems stand in the way of getting their friend to Jesus. That's taking action! There are people all around us who need to see Jesus. You probably can think of several right now. What actions can you take to make sure your friends know about Jesus? Take one step this week.

So you must never be ashamed
to tell others about our Lord.
2 Timothy 1:8, NLT

Teach Us to Pray

When you pray, do you feel you need to use special words or pray at a certain time? Sometimes it may be hard to know *how* to pray. But Jesus gave us some good advice.

Find out what he said...

Jesus taught the disciples about prayer. He told them, "When you pray, don't be like the people who only pretend to be good. They love to pray in front of everyone on street corners and in the synagogues where everyone can see them. The truth is, that is all the reward they will ever get. But when you pray, go away by yourself, shut the door behind you, and pray to your Father secretly. Then your Father, who knows all secrets, will reward you.

"When you pray, don't babble on and on as people of other religions do. They think their prayers are answered only by repeating their words again and again. Don't be like them, because your Father knows exactly what you need even before you ask him!" Jesus taught this prayer:

Our Father in Heaven,
may your name be honored.
May your kingdom come soon.
May your will be done here on Earth,
just as it is in Heaven.
Give us our food for today,
and forgive us our sins,

just as we have forgiven those who have sinned against us.

And don't let us give in to temptation, but rescue us from the evil one.

Jesus also said, "If you forgive those who sin against you, your heavenly Father will forgive you. But if you refuse to forgive others, your Father will not forgive your sins."

Story based on Matthew 6:5-15 as it appears in the New Living Translation®.

Let's talk about it...

When we pray, our attention should be on God. We don't need to think about people who may be listening. And we don't need to worry too much about the words we are using. Jesus gave us the Lord's Prayer as an example for our prayers. Remember that God always hears all of our prayers and answers them in the way that's best for us.

I love the LORD
because he hears and answers my prayers.
Psalm 116:1, NLT

A Show of Thanks

When someone does something really nice for us, it's natural to show that we appreciate it. In this story two people responded in very different ways to what Jesus had done for them.
Decide what made the difference...

Simon the Pharisee asked Jesus to come to his home for a meal. A certain sinful woman heard he was there and brought a beautiful jar filled with expensive perfume. Then she knelt behind Jesus at his feet. Her tears fell on his feet, and she wiped them off with her hair. Then she kept kissing his feet and putting perfume on them.

When Simon saw what was happening and who the woman was, he said to himself, "If God had really sent Jesus, he would know what kind of woman is touching him. She's a sinner!"

Then Jesus spoke up and answered Simon's thoughts by telling him this story: "A man loaned money to two people—five hundred pieces of silver to one and fifty pieces to the other. But neither of them could repay him, so he kindly forgave them both. Who do you suppose loved him more after that?"

Simon answered, "I suppose the one for whom he canceled the larger debt."

"That's right," Jesus said. Then he turned to the woman and said to Simon, "Look at this woman. When I entered your home, you didn't wash my feet. But this woman has washed my feet with her tears, wiped them

with her hair, and rubbed my feet with special perfume.
I tell you, her sins—and they are many—have been
forgiven, so she has shown me much love. But a person
who is forgiven little shows only a little love." Then
Jesus said to the woman, "Your sins are forgiven."

Story based on Luke 7:36-48 as it appears in the New Living Translation®.

Let's talk about it...

Jesus offered forgiveness to Simon and the woman.
Simon didn't think he needed it, but the woman knew
how much Jesus had forgiven her. And she responded
with love and thankfulness. When we remember how
many times we have sinned and been forgiven, we
realize how much God loves us. Then we respond with
love and thankfulness.

Oh, what joy for those whose disobedience is forgiven,
whose sins are put out of sight.

Romans 4:7, NLT

"Storm, Storm, Go Away"

Have you ever chanted, "Rain, rain, go away," when bad weather ruined your plans and you were forced indoors? The words may have been fun to say, but they didn't stop the rain. When Jesus told a storm to go away, though, the results he got were awesome.

Read about Jesus' amazing power...

As evening came, Jesus said to his disciples, "Let's cross to the other side of the lake." Jesus was already in the boat, so they started out. Jesus and the disciples left the crowds behind on the shore of the lake (although other boats followed them).

But soon a fierce storm arose. High waves began to break into the boat until it was nearly full of water. The disciples were very afraid of the storm.

During the storm, Jesus was sleeping at the back of the boat with his head on a cushion. Frantically the disciples woke him up, shouting, "Teacher, don't you even care that we are going to drown?"

When Jesus woke up, he scolded the wind and said to the water, "Quiet down!" Suddenly the wind stopped, and there was a great calm.

Then Jesus asked the disciples, "Why are you so afraid? Do you still not have faith in me?"

And the disciples were filled with surprise and said among themselves, "Who is this man, that even the wind and waves obey him?"

Story based on Mark 4:35-41 as it appears in the New Living Translation®.

Let's talk about it...

The disciples were terrified by the storm. Yet, when they woke Jesus up, they didn't really expect Jesus could do anything to help them. So they were amazed to see Jesus' power over the weather. That same power is here for us. No matter what kind of problem we face, Jesus can handle it. All we need to do is to ask and expect him to act.

You are the one who rules the oceans. When their waves rise in fearful storms, you subdue them.

Psalm 89:9, NLT

When you have something hard to do, how do you handle it? Do you give up right away? Or do you try to find someone to help you? This story is about some disciples who told Jesus, "We can't!" before they had even tried.

But look at how Jesus responded....

Jesus crossed over the Sea of Galilee with his disciples. A huge crowd kept following Jesus, because they saw him heal the sick. Then Jesus went up into the hills and sat down with his disciples around him.

Jesus saw the great crowd of people climbing the hills, looking for him. Turning to Philip, he asked, "Philip, where can we buy bread to feed all these people?" He was testing Philip, for Jesus already knew what he was going to do.

Philip replied, "We would never have enough money to feed all of them!"

Then Andrew, Simon Peter's brother, spoke up. "There's a young boy here with five loaves of bread and two fish. But what good is that with this huge crowd?"

"Tell everyone to sit down," Jesus ordered. So all of them—the men alone numbered five thousand—sat down on the grassy hillside. Then Jesus took the bread, gave thanks to God, and passed the bread out to the people. Afterward he did the same with the fish. And they all ate until they were full.

"Now gather the leftovers," Jesus told his disciples, "so that nothing is wasted." They had started out with

five loaves of bread, but they collected twelve baskets
filled with leftover bread that the people did not eat!

When the people saw this miracle, they exclaimed,
"Surely, Jesus is the prophet that we have been
expecting God to send!"

Story based on John 6:1-14 as it appears in the New Living Translation®.

Let's talk about it...

Philip looked at all the people on that hillside and said,
"Impossible!" Andrew found someone who had some
food, but he didn't think it would help much. Neither of
them thought about what *God* was able to do! When
you face a tough problem, don't give up. Ask God for
his help. Together, you'll even be able to tackle jobs that
seem impossible.

But with God everything is possible.
Matthew 19:26, NLT

Keep Your Eyes on Jesus

In order to hit a baseball, the rule is simple: Keep your eye on the ball. Do that, and you'll get a hit. In this story Peter needed to keep his eyes focused on one thing. Check it out...

Jesus made his disciples get into a boat and cross to the other side of the Sea of Galilee while he sent the crowds of people home. Afterward Jesus went up into the hills by himself to pray. Night fell while he was there alone. Meanwhile, the disciples were having trouble in the boat far away from land. A strong wind had risen, and they were fighting heavy waves.

About three o'clock in the morning Jesus came to the disciples. He was walking on the water. When the disciples saw him, they screamed in terror because they thought that he was a ghost. But Jesus spoke to them at once. "It's all right," he said. "I am here! Don't be afraid."

Then Peter called to him, "Lord, if it's really you, tell me to walk on the water and come to you."

"All right, come," Jesus said.

So Peter went over the side of the boat and walked on the water toward Jesus. But when Peter looked around at the high waves, he was terrified and began to sink. "Save me, Lord!" Peter shouted.

Instantly Jesus reached out his hand and grabbed Peter. "You don't have much faith," Jesus said. "Why did you doubt me?" And when they climbed back into the boat, the wind stopped.

Then the disciples worshiped Jesus and exclaimed, "You really are the Son of God!"

Story based on Matthew 14:22-33 as it appears in the New Living Translation®.

Let's talk about it...

When Peter kept his eyes on Jesus, he stayed afloat. As soon as Peter looked down and saw the high waves, he got scared and began to sink. We may never walk on water, but we will walk through tough times. When we do, we need to remember: Don't focus on your troubles. Keep your eyes on Jesus. Have faith that he'll guide you through.

We do this by keeping our eyes on Jesus, on whom our faith depends from start to finish.
Hebrews 12:2, NLT

Who Do You Say I Am?

How would you describe Jesus? Would you repeat what you have heard others say? Or would you talk about your friendship with him? In this story Jesus asks the disciples to decide what they think of him.
Listen to what they said...

One day as Jesus was alone, praying, he came over to his disciples and asked them, "Who do people say I am?"

"Well," they answered, "some say John the Baptist, some say Elijah, and others say you are one of the other prophets from long ago who has risen from the dead."

Then Jesus asked them, "Who do you say I am?"

Peter replied, "You are the Messiah sent from God!"

Jesus warned them not to tell anyone about this. "For I, the Son of Man, must suffer many terrible things," he said. "The leaders, the leading priests, and the teachers of religious law will turn against me. I will be killed, but three days later I will be raised from the dead."

Then Jesus said to the crowd, "If any of you wants to be my follower, you must put aside your selfish desires, be willing to die for me, and follow me. If you try to keep your life for yourself, you will lose it. But if you give up your life for me, you will find true life. Because how will it help you if you gain the whole world but end up losing your own soul? If a person is ashamed of me and my message, I, the Son of Man, will be ashamed of that person. I will return in my glory and in the glory of the Father and the holy angels. And I

promise you that some of you standing here right now will not die before you see the Kingdom of God."

Story based on Luke 9:18-27 as it appears in the New Living Translation®.

Let's talk about it...

Jesus wanted to find out what the disciples thought about who he was. At first the disciples repeated what other people had said about Jesus. But then Jesus asked them to give their own answer. Put yourself in the disciples' place—how would you answer? It's not your parents' answer or your friends' answer. Jesus wants to know: *"Who do you say I am?"*

For if you confess with your mouth that Jesus is Lord and believe in your heart that God raised him from the dead, you will be saved.

Romans 10:9, NLT

Jesus Shines On

When you read the Bible, are there some parts that you don't understand? Don't worry. You're not alone! The disciples had a hard time understanding what Jesus taught, too.

This story is about one of those times...

Six days later Jesus took Peter, James, and John, and led them up a high mountain. As the men watched, Jesus changed so that his face shone like the sun, and his clothing became dazzling white. Suddenly, Moses and Elijah appeared and began talking with Jesus. Peter blurted out, "Lord, this is wonderful! If you want me to, I'll make three shrines, one for you, one for Moses, and one for Elijah."

But even as he said it, a bright cloud came over them, and a voice from the cloud said, "This is my beloved Son, and I am very pleased with him. Listen to him." The disciples were terrified and fell face down on the ground.

Jesus came over and touched the disciples. "Get up," he said, "don't be afraid." And when they looked, they saw only Jesus with them. As they went down the mountain, Jesus commanded them, "Don't tell anyone what you have seen until I have been raised from the dead."

His disciples asked, "Why do the teachers of religious law insist that Elijah must come back before the Messiah comes?"

Jesus replied, "Elijah is indeed coming first to set everything in order. But I tell you, he has already

come. But people didn't recognize him, and he was badly mistreated. And soon the Son of Man will also suffer at their hands." Then the disciples knew he had been speaking of John the Baptist.

Story based on Matthew 17:1-13 as it appears in the New Living Translation®.

Let's talk about it...

Peter, James, and John were confused by what they saw and heard. Whenever we are confused by spiritual mysteries, the best thing to do is talk to God. Tell him what you don't understand and ask for help. The Holy Spirit can help us understand God's Word and how we are to live as God's followers.

The Holy Spirit . . . will teach you everything and will remind you of everything I myself have told you.

John 14:26, NLT

Who Is My Neighbor?

It's easy to do something nice for a friend. But how about sharing with someone who calls you names? Or how about helping a person who has hurt you? That's tough to do.

Jesus had something to say about whom we should love...

One day an expert in religious law stood up to test Jesus by asking him this question: "Teacher, what must I do to receive eternal life?"

Jesus replied, "What does the law of Moses say?"

The man answered, "'You must love the Lord your God with all your heart, soul, strength, and mind.' And, 'Love your neighbor as yourself.'"

"Right!" Jesus told him. "Do this and you will live!"

Then the man asked Jesus, "Who is my neighbor?"

Jesus answered with a story: A Jewish man was traveling from Jerusalem to Jericho and was attacked by robbers. They stole his clothes and money. They beat him up and left him half dead by the road.

By chance a Jewish priest came along; but when he saw the man lying there, he crossed to the other side of the road and passed him by. A temple assistant walked by and looked at him lying there, but he also passed by.

Then a hated Samaritan came along, and when he saw the man, he felt very sorry for the hurt man. The Samaritan soothed his wounds with medicine, and he bandaged them. Then he put the man on his own

donkey and took him to an inn, where he took care of him. The next day he gave the innkeeper money and told him to take care of the man.

"Now who was a neighbor to the man who was attacked by robbers?" Jesus asked.

The man replied, "The one who felt sorry and helped him."

Then Jesus said, "Yes, now go and do the same."

Story based on Luke 10:25-37 as it appears in the New Living Translation®.

Let's talk about it...

In Bible times Jews and Samaritans did not like each other. But in Jesus' story, a Samaritan is the only one who helps the Jewish man on the side of the road. To be good neighbors, we must love everyone who needs it—not just our friends. Jesus says that loving others— friends and enemies—is one way we show others that we love God.

The whole law can be summed up in this one command: "Love your neighbor as yourself."
Galatians 5:14, NLT

God's Great Love

Whom do you think God loves? Someone who tries to do the right thing all the time, or someone who messes up all the time? Jesus told a story to show that God always loves us, no matter what we do.

Look at what Jesus says...

Jesus told the religious teachers this story: "A man had two sons. The younger son told his father, 'I want my share of everything now, instead of waiting until you die.' So his father agreed to divide his wealth between his sons.

"A few days later this younger son packed all his belongings and traveled to a distant land. He wasted all his money on wild living. About the time his money ran out, the land also ran out of food, and he began to starve. So he asked a local farmer to hire him to feed his pigs. The boy became so hungry that even the pods he was feeding the pigs looked good to him. When no one would give him anything to eat, he decided to go back home.

"So he returned home to his father. And while he was still a long distance away, his father saw him coming. Filled with love and tenderness, he ran to his son, hugged him, and kissed him. His son said to him, 'Father, I have sinned against both Heaven and you, and I am no longer worthy of being called your son.'

"But his father said to the servants, 'Quick! Bring the finest robe in the house and put it on him. Get a ring for his finger, and sandals for his feet. And kill

the calf we have been fattening in the pen. We must celebrate with a feast, for this son of mine was dead and has now returned to life. He was lost, but now he is found.' So the party began."

Story based on Luke 15:11-24 as it appears in the New Living Translation®.

Let's talk about it...

Just like the father in Jesus' story, God always loves us, even when we don't deserve it. When we tell God that we want to stop sinning and live as he wants, the Bible tells us that all of Heaven celebrates! Whether our sins are big or small, we need God's forgiveness. And God is always ready to give it to us.

But God showed his great love for us by sending Christ to die for us while we were still sinners.

Romans 5:8, NLT

The Wise Choice

If you are like most kids, your days are filled with school, homework, chores, and lots of fun activities. Those things are good and important for us to do. But in this story, one sister discovered that there is something even *more* important than all of those other things.

Check out her discovery...

Jesus and the disciples were on their way to Jerusalem. They came to the village of Bethany where a woman named Martha welcomed them into her home. She lived there with her sister, Mary, and their brother, Lazarus.

Her sister, Mary, was sitting at the Lord's feet, listening to what he taught. But Martha was worrying about the big dinner she was preparing. So Martha did not spend time with Jesus because she thought that there were too many other things to do.

Martha came to Jesus and said, "Lord, doesn't it seem unfair to you that my sister just sits here while I do all the work? Tell her to come and help me."

But the Lord said to her, "My dear Martha, you are so upset over all these details! There is really only one thing worth being concerned about—one thing that is more important than everything else. Mary has discovered it—and I won't take it away from her."

Story based on Luke 10:38-42 as it appears in the New Living Translation®.

Did you hear what Jesus told Martha? *There is really only one thing worth being concerned about.* We need to do our daily chores, homework, and other activities. But we should always remember what's most important. And that is learning about Jesus and what he did for us. We don't need to get upset about the little details like Martha did. Why? Because God promises that he will give us all we need from day to day if we live for him. We need to be more like Mary and find time to spend with Jesus every day. That's how to make sure we're living for him.

And he will give you all you need from day to day if you live for him and make the Kingdom of God your primary concern.

Matthew 6:33, NLT

Just Kids

Sometimes, the hardest thing about being a kid is that people treat you like one! In this story Jesus had a few words for his disciples who tried to stop some kids from "bothering" him. Jesus showed that kids are much more important than the disciples realized!

Listen to what Jesus said...

One day some parents brought their children to Jesus so he could touch them and bless them. But the disciples told the parents to stop bringing their children. They did not want the children to bother Jesus.

But when Jesus saw what was happening, he was very unhappy with his disciples. He said to the disciples, "Let the children come to me. Don't stop them! For the Kingdom of God belongs to people who are like these children.

"I promise you, anyone who doesn't have their kind of faith will never get into the Kingdom of God." Then he took the children into his arms and placed his hands on their heads and blessed them.

Story based on Mark 10:13-16 as it appears in the New Living Translation®.

Let's talk about it...

Jesus' disciples didn't think children were important enough to take up Jesus' time. But in Jesus' Kingdom, everyone is important—especially kids! Everyone, he said, should have the trusting faith of a child. You will grow and change a lot in the coming years. But no matter how old you are, you will never outgrow the kind of faith that trusts and loves God.

I assure you, unless you turn from your sins
and become as little children,
you will never get into the Kingdom of Heaven.

Matthew 18:3, NLT

Can You Hear Me Now?

What's the best way to get someone's attention in a big crowd? Jumping up and down? Yelling in your loudest voice? A beggar who was blind shouted to get Jesus' attention even though others told him to be quiet. But he wouldn't let them stop him from getting to Jesus.
See what happened when Jesus heard him...

Jesus and his disciples reached Jericho. Later, as Jesus and his disciples were leaving town, a great crowd was following them. A beggar who was blind named Bartimaeus, was sitting beside the road as Jesus and the disciples were walking by. When Bartimaeus heard that Jesus from Nazareth was nearby, he began to shout out, "Jesus, Son of David, have mercy on me!"

"Be quiet!" some of the people yelled at him.

But he only shouted louder, "Son of David, have mercy on me!"

When Jesus heard him, he stopped and said, "Tell him to come here."

So they called the blind man. "Cheer up," they said. "Come on, he's calling you!" Bartimaeus threw aside his coat, jumped up, and came to Jesus.

"What do you want me to do for you?" Jesus asked.

"Teacher," the blind man said, "I want to see!"

And Jesus said to him, "Go your way. Your faith has healed you." And instantly the blind man could see! Then he followed Jesus down the road.

Story based on Mark 10:46-52 as it appears in the New Living Translation®.

Let's talk about it...

Bartimaeus knew Jesus could help him, and Bartimaeus wasn't going to keep quiet about asking. Sometimes people might want to stop us from asking for Jesus' help, too. They might say that Jesus can't hear us. Or they might say that we aren't important enough for Jesus to help us. We can't be discouraged from calling out to Jesus. He hears us and will help us.

Listen! The LORD is not too weak to save you, and he is not becoming deaf. He can hear you when you call.

Isaiah 59:1, NLT

Jesus Sees Zacchaeus

People do some crazy things to get a look at someone famous. What if you really wanted to see someone famous, and it turned out that the person really wanted to see you?

That's what happened to Zacchaeus in this story...

Jesus entered Jericho and made his way through the town. There was a man there named Zacchaeus. He was one of the most important Jews in the Roman tax-collecting business. He had become very rich. Zacchaeus tried to get a look at Jesus, but he was too short to see over the crowds. So he ran ahead and climbed a sycamore tree beside the road, so he could watch for Jesus from there.

When Jesus came by, he looked up at Zacchaeus and called him by name. "Zacchaeus!" he said. "Quick, come down! I must be a guest in your home today."

Zacchaeus quickly climbed down and took Jesus to his house. Zacchaeus was very excited. But the crowds were upset. "He has gone to be the guest of a sinner," they grumbled.

Meanwhile, Zacchaeus stood there and said to the Lord, "I will give half of my wealth to the poor, Lord, and if I have charged people too much tax money, I will give them back four times as much as I took!"

Jesus said, "Salvation has come to this home today, for Zacchaeus really is a son of Abraham. And I, the

Son of Man, have come to find and save those like Zacchaeus who are lost."

Story based on Luke 19:1-10 as it appears in the New Living Translation®.

Let's talk about it...

Zacchaeus probably thought that he was looking for Jesus when he climbed that tree. Sometimes we think like Zacchaeus did. It may seem that we have to work really hard to find Jesus. But Jesus is always looking for us. Jesus wants to love us, save us when we are lost, and forgive our sins. We don't need to hunt for Jesus; he is always with us.

I love all who love me.
Those who search for me will surely find me.

Proverbs 8:17, NLT

Three Cheers for Jesus!

When a sports team is winning, the fans cheer and root them on. But when the team starts to lose, some so-called fans start to complain or even boo. They stop supporting the team. We call those people fair-weather fans.

Jesus met his own fair-weather fans...

As Jesus and the disciples came near Jerusalem, they came to the town of Bethphage on the Mount of Olives. Jesus sent two of the disciples on ahead. "Go into the village over there," he said, "and you will see a donkey tied there, with its colt beside it. Untie them and bring them here. If anyone asks what you are doing, just say, 'The Lord needs them,' and he will immediately send them."

When this was done, it made the words of the prophet come true: "Tell the people of Israel, 'Look, your King is coming to you. He is humble, riding on a donkey—even on a donkey's colt.'"

The two disciples did as Jesus said. They brought the animals to Jesus and threw their coats over the colt, and then Jesus sat on it.

As Jesus and the disciples came to the city, most of the crowd spread their coats on the road ahead of Jesus. Other people cut branches from the trees and spread them on the road.

Jesus was in the center of the parade. The crowds all around him were shouting, "Praise God for the Son of David! Bless the one who comes in the name of the Lord! Praise God in highest heaven!"

The whole city of Jerusalem was excited as he entered. "Who is this?" they asked.

And the crowds replied, "It's Jesus, the prophet from Nazareth in Galilee."

Story based on Matthew 21:1-11 as it appears in the New Living Translation®.

Let's talk about it...

The people of Jerusalem got carried away by a thrilling moment. But in just a few days, the same crowds who had been cheering for Jesus would scream and yell about putting Jesus to death. Our love for Jesus should not depend on what other people do. We should love and praise Jesus whether we're in a worship service or alone at school. Are you a fair-weather follower or one of Jesus' loyal fans?

I have taken a stand, and I will publicly praise the LORD.
Psalm 26:12, NLT

Not in God's House

Would you ever skateboard in a library? Or play football in a grocery store? No way! That's not what those places are made for. In this story the Jewish people had been using God's Temple as a store instead of a place to worship God.

Look what Jesus did when he walked in...

Jesus entered the Temple and began to drive out the merchants and their customers. He knocked over the tables of the men who were exchanging different kinds of money. And he knocked down the stalls of the people selling doves.

Jesus said, "The Scriptures say, 'My Temple will be called a place of prayer,' but you have turned it into a hangout for robbers!"

People who were blind or disabled came to Jesus, and he healed them there in the Temple. The leading priests and the teachers of religious law saw these wonderful miracles. They heard even the little children in the Temple shouting, "Praise God for the Son of David." But the priests and teachers were angry, so they asked Jesus, "Do you hear what these children are saying?"

"Yes," Jesus replied. "Haven't you ever read the Scriptures? For they say, 'You have taught children and infants to give you praise.'"

Then he left the city and went to Bethany, where he stayed overnight.

Story based on Matthew 21:12-17 as it appears in the New Living Translation®.

Let's talk about it...

God's house is supposed to be a special place to worship. But people were acting like it was an ordinary market. When Jesus came, he told the merchants to get out of the Temple. Then Jesus started teaching and healing people. Our church is God's house. When we worship, we are visiting with God and hearing what God has to say.

Who may climb the mountain of the LORD? Who may stand in his holy place? Only those whose hands and hearts are pure.

Psalm 24:3-4, NLT

A Gift from the Heart

How do you show respect to favorite teachers or coaches? Maybe you listen to them and respond respectfully or do something special for them. In this story a woman showed Jesus a great deal of respect. Discover what she did...

It was now two days before the Passover celebration and the Festival of Unleavened Bread. The leading priests and the teachers of religious law were still looking for a chance to capture Jesus secretly. They wanted to kill him.

Meanwhile, Jesus was in Bethany at the home of Simon, a man who had leprosy. During supper, a woman came in with a beautiful jar of expensive perfume. She opened the jar and poured the perfume over Jesus' head. Some of the people at the table were angry. "Why was this expensive perfume wasted?" they asked. "She could have sold it for a large amount of money and given the money to the poor!" And they scolded her harshly.

But Jesus answered, "Leave her alone. Why punish her for doing such a good thing to me? You will always have the poor with you, and you can help them whenever you want. But I will not be here with you much longer. She has done what she could. She has even prepared my body for burial ahead of time. I tell you, wherever the good news is preached, this woman's actions will be talked about."

Then Judas Iscariot, one of the twelve disciples, went to the leading priests and planned to give Jesus to them. The leading priests were delighted when they heard why Judas had come. They promised him a reward. So Judas began looking for the right time and place to betray Jesus.

Story based on Mark 14:1-11 as it appears in the New Living Translation®.

Let's talk about it...

The woman in this story showed Jesus love and respect by giving him a very expensive gift. Jesus accepted the woman's gift because it showed how much she loved Jesus. It doesn't matter what we give Jesus. What matters is that our gifts come from our hearts. How can you show Jesus your love and respect today?

I will bring honor to your name in every generation. Therefore, the nations will praise you forever and ever.

Psalm 45:17, NLT

Wash My Feet?

You probably aren't used to having people wash your feet. But when Jesus lived on Earth, servants always did that for their masters. In this story, though, Jesus, the teacher, washed his disciples' feet.
Find out how they reacted...

Before the Passover celebration, Jesus knew that he would return to his Father in Heaven. So he showed the disciples how much he loved them. When it was time for supper, Jesus got up from the table and took off his robe. He wrapped a towel around his waist and poured water into a basin. Then he began to wash the disciples' feet.

When Jesus came to Simon Peter, Peter said to him, "Lord, why are you going to wash my feet?"

Jesus answered, "You don't understand now why I am doing it, but someday you will."

Peter said, "You will never wash my feet!"

Jesus answered, "But if I don't wash you, you won't belong to me."

Simon Peter exclaimed, "Then wash all of me!"

Jesus replied, "A person who has bathed all over does not need to wash, except for the feet, to be entirely clean. And you are clean."

After washing their feet, Jesus put on his robe and asked, "Do you understand what I was doing? You call me 'teacher' and 'Lord,' and you are right, because it is true. And since I, the Lord and teacher, have washed your feet, you ought to wash each other's feet. I have

given you an example to follow. Do as I have done to you. How true it is that a servant is not greater than the master. Nor are messengers more important than the one who sends them. You know these things—now do them! That is the way to be happy.

Story based on John 13:1-17 as it appears in the New Living Translation®.

Let's talk about it...

The disciples were shocked when Jesus took the place of a servant and washed their feet. Jesus was teaching his disciples—and us—a very important lesson. Jesus wants us to follow his example and serve others. Serving people is a great way to show that we love them and want to help them.

And all of you, serve each other in humility.
I Peter 5:5, NLT

A Very Special Supper

What do you know about the Lord's Supper? Do you know why it is celebrated in church? This story is about the first celebration of the Lord's Supper.

Examine the important things Jesus told his disciples...

The disciples came to Jesus and asked, "Where do you want us to have the Passover supper?"

"As you go into the city," he told them, "you will see a certain man. Tell him, 'The teacher says, My time has come, and I will eat the Passover meal with my disciples here.'" So the disciples did as Jesus told them.

When it was evening, Jesus sat down at the table with the twelve disciples. While they were eating, he said, "The truth is, one of you will turn against me."

The disciples were very upset. One by one they began to ask him, "I'm not the one, am I, Lord?"

Jesus answered, "I must die, as the Scriptures said long ago. But how terrible it will be for my betrayer. It would be better for him if he had never been born!"

Judas, the one who would betray him, also asked, "Teacher, I'm not the one, am I?"

And Jesus told him, "You have said it yourself."

Then Jesus took a loaf of bread and asked God's blessing on it. He broke it in pieces and gave it to the disciples, saying, "Take it and eat it, for this is my body." And he took a cup of wine and gave thanks to God for it. He gave it to them and said, "Each of you

drink from it, for this is my blood. There is now a new
agreement between God and his people. My blood is
poured out to forgive the sins of many. Mark my
words—I will not drink wine again until the day I
drink it new with you in my Father's Kingdom."

Story based on Matthew 26:17-29 as it appears in the New Living Translation®.

Let's talk about it...

The Lord's Supper has been an important part of worship
since the beginning of the church. The words Jesus spoke
at the first supper are often repeated when the Lord's
Supper is celebrated. Those words remind us that our sins
are forgiven because Jesus was willing to die for us to fulfill
God's plan. That certainly is something to celebrate, isn't it?

For every time you eat this bread
and drink this cup, you are announcing the Lord's death
until he comes again.
1 Corinthians 11:26, NLT

Jesus Pays the Highest Price

When someone does something mean and hurtful, it can be hard to forgive that person. But God offers forgiveness to all people for *all* the wrong things they do every day.

Check out what Jesus was willing to do for our forgiveness...

After Jesus had been arrested, the men of the council took Jesus to Pilate, the Roman governor.

So Pilate asked Jesus, "Are you the king of the Jews?"

Jesus answered, "Yes, it is as you say."

Pilate said to the leading priests and to the crowd, "I find nothing wrong with this man!"

Pilate sent him to Herod Antipas, and Herod was happy to see Jesus because he wanted to see a miracle. He asked Jesus many questions, but Jesus would not answer. Herod and his soldiers began to make fun of Jesus. Then they put a royal robe on him and sent him back to Pilate.

Then Pilate called together the religious leaders along with the people. He gave his decision. "This man has done nothing to die for. I will have him beaten, and then I will let him go."

Then a mighty roar rose from the crowd, and all together they shouted, "Kill him, and release Barabbas to us!" (Barabbas was in prison for murder and for causing trouble for the government.) Pilate argued with them, but the crowd shouted louder and louder. So Pilate sentenced Jesus to die, and he let Barabbas go.

As they led Jesus away, Simon of Cyrene was forced to follow Jesus and carry his cross. Great crowds trailed along behind, including many sad, crying women.

Two other men, both criminals, were crucified with Jesus that day.

Story based on Luke 23:1-32 as it appears in the New Living Translation®.

Let's talk about it...

Jesus didn't die because the people in this story wanted to kill him. There was a bigger plan. Jesus willingly went to the cross so that *all* sins of *all* people could be forgiven. Jesus died for our sins—even though we were born hundreds of years after he died. Can you imagine? Take time to thank God for the wonderful thing Jesus did for us.

When we were utterly helpless, Christ came at just the right time and died for us sinners.

Romans 5:6, NLT

Jesus Is Alive!

Everyone knows that dead people don't get up and walk away. So it must have been quite a shock for Mary and her friends when they went to Jesus' tomb and found it empty. Where could his body have gone?
Read what the angels told them...

Very early on Sunday morning some women came to Jesus' tomb, taking the spices they had prepared. They found that the stone covering the opening of the tomb had been rolled away. So they went in, but they couldn't find the body of the Lord Jesus. The women were puzzled, trying to think what could have happened to it.

Suddenly, two men appeared to them, wearing dazzling robes. The women were terrified and bowed low before them. Then the men asked, "Why are you looking in a tomb for someone who is alive? He isn't here! He has risen from the dead! Don't you remember what he told you back in Galilee—that the Son of Man must be turned over to sinful men and be crucified, and that he would rise again the third day?"

Then the women remembered that Jesus had said this. So they rushed back to tell his eleven disciples—and everyone else—what had happened. The women who went to the tomb were Mary Magdalene, Joanna, Mary the mother of James, and several others. They told the apostles what had happened. But the story sounded like nonsense, so the apostles didn't believe it.

However, Peter ran to the tomb to look. Stooping, he looked in and saw the empty grave clothes; then he went home again, wondering what had happened.

Story based on Luke 24:1-12 as it appears in the New Living Translation®.

Let's talk about it...

The angels' message was awesome—Jesus had risen from the dead. He was alive! All of Jesus' life was amazing. But Jesus' resurrection proved that he even has power over death. Because we believe Jesus is alive, we know that we will not stay dead either. We also will be raised from the dead to live with Jesus forever in Heaven. And that's good news!

We know that the same God who raised our Lord Jesus will also raise us with Jesus and present us to himself along with you.

2 Corinthians 4:14, NLT

A Hopeless Situation?

When everything is going wrong, it's easy to lose hope. In this story two of Jesus' followers were so upset by Jesus' death that they forgot some very important details.

See what happened...

Two of Jesus' followers were walking to the village of Emmaus. Suddenly, Jesus himself began walking beside them. But they didn't recognize him.

"You seem to be having an interesting talk," Jesus said. "What are you talking about?"

Then one of them said, "You must be the only person in Jerusalem who hasn't heard about all the things that have happened there the last few days."

"What things?" Jesus asked.

"The things that happened to Jesus, the man from Nazareth," they said. "He was a prophet who did wonderful miracles. But our religious leaders crucified him. We thought he was the Messiah who had come to rescue Israel. That all happened three days ago. Then some women who were at his tomb early this morning said his body was missing. They said angels told them Jesus is alive!"

Then Jesus told them, "You are such foolish people! You find it so hard to believe all that the prophets wrote in the Scriptures." Then Jesus explained what all the Scriptures said about himself.

The men begged Jesus to stay the night with them, since it was getting late. As they sat down to eat, Jesus

took a loaf of bread, asked God's blessing on it, broke it, then gave it to them. Suddenly, they recognized him. And at that moment he disappeared!

Within the hour they were on their way to Jerusalem, where the followers of Jesus were gathered. When they arrived, the other followers of Jesus said, "The Lord has really risen! He appeared to Peter!"

Story based on Luke 24:13-34 as it appears in the New Living Translation®.

Let's talk about it...

These disciples were so sad because they had lost hope. They didn't recognize that Jesus was right there with them. When we are sad, we can easily lose hope. We might stop expecting God to do good things. But God gives us hope when he promises to always be with us and help us. Count on God's promise!

So I pray that God, who gives you hope, will keep
you happy and full of peace as you believe in him.
May you overflow with hope
through the power of the Holy Spirit.
Romans 15:13, NLT

I'll Believe It When I See It!

Do you usually believe what people tell you? Or do you want them to prove that what they say is true? In this story Thomas wasn't ready to believe what the other disciples told him was true about Jesus. Look at the kind of proof Thomas got...

One of the disciples, Thomas (nicknamed the Twin), was not with the other disciples when Jesus appeared to them. They told Thomas, "We have seen the Lord!" But Thomas said, "I won't believe it unless I see the nail wounds in his hands, put my fingers into them, and place my hand into the wound in his side."

Eight days later the disciples were together again, and this time Thomas was with them. The doors to the room they were in were locked. But suddenly Jesus was standing in the room with them. Jesus said, "Peace be with you." Then he said to Thomas, "Put your finger here and see my hands. Put your hand into the wound in my side. Don't be without faith any longer. Believe!"

"My Lord and my God!" Thomas exclaimed.

Then Jesus told Thomas, "You believe because you have seen me. Blessed are those who haven't seen me and believe anyway."

Jesus' disciples saw him do many other miracles besides the ones written in this book. But these miracles are written so that you may believe that Jesus is the Messiah, the Son of God. By believing in him you will have life.

Story based on John 20:24-31 as it appears in the New Living Translation®.

It may seem strange that Thomas would think that his friends were tricking him about something so serious. But rising from the dead is not normal, and Thomas needed proof that Jesus was alive. Jesus gave Thomas the proof he wanted. Then Jesus said that people who could believe without seeing are blessed. We are those people. We might not be able to see Jesus in person, but in God's Word—the Bible—we have the proof we need to believe.

But these are written so that you may believe that Jesus is the Messiah, the Son of God, and that by believing in him you will have life.

John 20:31, NLT

That's Got to Be Jesus!

Can you tell who someone is even if he's wearing a mask? Sometimes the best way to identify people is to watch what they do. People usually act the same even if they look different than they usually do. The disciples looked for those kinds of clues in this story...

Later Jesus appeared again to the disciples beside the Sea of Galilee. Several of the disciples were there— Simon Peter, Thomas, Nathanael, the sons of Zebedee, and two other disciples.

Simon Peter said, "I'm going fishing."

"We'll come, too," they all said. So they went out in the boat, but they didn't catch anything all night.

At dawn Jesus was standing on the beach, but the disciples couldn't see who he was. He called out, "Friends, have you caught any fish?"

"No," they answered.

Then he said, "Throw out your net on the right-hand side of the boat, and you'll get plenty of fish!" So they did, and their nets became too heavy to lift.

Then the disciple whom Jesus loved said, "It is the Lord!" When Peter heard this, he jumped into the water and swam ashore.

When the others got there in the boat, Jesus said, "Bring some of the fish you've just caught." So Peter dragged the net to the shore.

"Now come and have some breakfast!" Jesus said. And no one asked him if he really was the Lord because they were sure of it. Then Jesus served them the bread and the fish. This was the third time Jesus had appeared to his disciples since he had been raised from the dead.

Story based on John 21:1-14 as it appears in the New Living Translation®.

Let's talk about it...

The disciples may have had a hard time recognizing Jesus after his resurrection. But Jesus' fishing advice gave "the disciple Jesus loved" a big clue. Sometimes we can't tell that God is near just by looking. A great way to recognize God is by what he does. Whenever people are loving each other and turning away from sin, God is at work in their lives.

Your love for one another will prove to the world that you are my disciples.

John 13:35, NLT

Time for a Change

As you get older, life changes. Your interests change. Looks change. Sometimes, even your friends change. In this story the disciples discovered that they were in for a big change in how Jesus would be with them.

Check it out...

During the forty days after Jesus rose from the dead, he appeared to the apostles from time to time. He proved to them in many ways that he was really alive.

In one of these meetings, Jesus was eating with the apostles. He told them, "Do not leave Jerusalem until the Father sends you what he promised. John baptized with water, but soon you will be baptized with the Holy Spirit. When the Holy Spirit has come upon you, you will receive power and will tell people about me everywhere—in Jerusalem, all over Judea, in Samaria, and to faraway places on the earth."

It was not long after Jesus said this that he was taken up into the sky. While the apostles were watching, he disappeared into a cloud. As they were straining their eyes to see him, two white-robed men suddenly stood there with them. They said, "Why are you standing here staring at the sky? Jesus has been taken into heaven. And someday, just as you saw him go, he will return!"

The apostles were at the Mount of Olives when this happened, so they walked the half mile back to

Jerusalem. Then they went to the upstairs room of the house where they were staying.

The apostles met together all the time for prayer, along with Mary the mother of Jesus, several other women, and the brothers of Jesus.

Story based on Acts 1:3-14 as it appears in the New Living Translation®.

Let's talk about it...

When Jesus rose into the sky, the disciples kept staring up after him. After this, Jesus would not be walking around with them anymore. Instead, Jesus would live *inside* the disciples. The Holy Spirit would help the disciples follow Jesus even though they couldn't see him. Jesus lives in our hearts too, and the Holy Spirit helps us follow him.

And because you . . . have become his children, God has sent the Spirit of his Son into your hearts, and now you can call God your dear Father.

Galatians 4:6, NLT

The Power to Speak

When a friend asks you about Jesus, do you have trouble answering? Finding the right words isn't always easy. The disciples discovered an unusual source that gave them the power to talk about their faith.
Discover the source of that power...

On Pentecost, seven weeks after Jesus' resurrection, the believers were all together. Suddenly, there was a sound like the roaring of a mighty windstorm, and it filled the house where they were. Then, what looked like flames appeared and rested on each of them. And everyone was filled with the Holy Spirit. He gave them the ability to speak other languages.

Godly Jews from many nations were in Jerusalem at that time. When they heard the sound, they came running to see what it was. They were surprised to hear the believers speaking their languages.

"How can this be?" they exclaimed. "We are from all over the world and we all hear these people from Galilee speaking in our own languages about the wonderful things God has done!"

Then Peter shouted to the crowd, "Listen carefully, all of you! Hundreds of years ago the prophet Joel said this would happen: 'In the last days, God said, I will pour out my Spirit upon all people.'

"People of Israel, listen! God was with Jesus of Nazareth by doing wonderful miracles through him, as you well know. But God knew what you would do.

With the help of wicked people, you murdered him. However, God raised him back to life again, for death could not hold him."

Those who believed what Peter said were baptized. They joined with the other believers to spend time studying the apostles' teaching. They liked being together to share in the Lord's Supper and in prayer.

Story based on Acts 2:1-42 as it appears in the New Living Translation®.

Let's talk about it...

Imagine being able to speak in different languages! The Holy Spirit gave the disciples the power to speak to *everybody* about Jesus—no matter what language they spoke. The Holy Spirit will give us the power and the words we need to speak to our friends about Jesus. Just ask God.

But when the Holy Spirit has come upon you,
you will receive power and will tell people about me
everywhere—in Jerusalem, throughout Judea,
in Samaria, and to the ends of the earth.

Acts 1:8, NLT

Changed in a Flash

Most of us change slowly as time passes and we grow older. It's not normal for somebody's life to change completely in one moment. But Saul's life changed in a flash.

Discover the difference one moment made...

When Saul was traveling to Damascus to destroy Jesus' followers, a bright light from heaven beamed down upon him! He fell to the ground and heard a voice call, "Saul! Why do you hurt me?"

"Who are you, sir?" Saul asked.

And the voice replied, "I am Jesus who you are hurting! Now go into the city, and you will be told what to do."

As Saul got up, he found that he was blind. So his friends led him to Damascus.

The Lord spoke to a believer in Damascus named Ananias, calling, "Ananias! Go to the house of Judas and ask for Saul."

"But, Lord," exclaimed Ananias, "I've heard about the terrible things this man has done to the believers!"

But the Lord said, "Do what I say. I have chosen Saul to take my message to many people."

When Ananias laid his hands on Saul, Saul was filled with the Holy Spirit. Scales fell from Saul's eyes, and he could see. Then he got up and was baptized.

Saul stayed with the believers in Damascus for a few days. And he began preaching about Jesus.

Everyone was amazed and asked, "Isn't this the same man who wanted to hurt Jesus' followers?"

Saul's preaching became more and more powerful, and many Jews in Damascus believed that Jesus was the Messiah. After a while some Jewish leaders decided to kill Saul. But some of the other believers helped Saul escape through an opening in the city wall.

Story based on Acts 9:1-25 as it appears in the New Living Translation®.

Let's talk about it...

Everyone was amazed by how Saul had changed. Saul had come to Damascus to put Christians in jail, but suddenly he was one of them! When we get to know Jesus, we often need to make big changes in our lives so that Jesus can be in charge. How did you change when you first believed in Jesus as your Savior? How is Jesus still changing you?

Those who become Christians become new persons. They are not the same anymore, for the old life is gone. A new life has begun!

2 Corinthians 5:17, NLT

Come One, Come All

Have you ever been left out of an activity or a group of friends? Being left out really hurts. The Jewish people didn't want anyone who was not Jewish in the church. But God showed Peter that anybody can be his follower...

Cornelius was a Roman army officer who believed in God, as did his entire household. One afternoon an angel of God appeared to Cornelius.

The angel said to him, "Send some men to Joppa to find Simon Peter. He is staying with a man near the shore who works with leather. Ask him to visit you."

As soon as the angel left, Cornelius sent two of his household servants and a soldier to Joppa.

As Cornelius's messengers were nearing the city, Peter was praying. He saw a vision. Something like a large sheet with animals on it was let down by its four corners. Then a voice said, "Get up, kill, and eat."

Peter said, "I have never eaten anything not allowed by Jewish law."

The voice spoke again, "If God says something is allowed, don't say it isn't."

Peter was confused, but just then the Holy Spirit said, "Three men have come to find you. Go with them, for I have sent them."

So Peter went with them to Joppa.

Cornelius, his relatives, and close friends were waiting to meet Peter.

Peter told them, "It is against Jewish law for me to enter a non-Jewish home. But God has shown me that I should never think of anyone as impure. I see now that God treats everyone the same. He accepts everyone who believes in him."

Even as Peter was talking, the Holy Spirit came upon all who had heard the message. So Peter baptized them in the name of Jesus Christ.

Story based on Acts 10:1-48 as it appears in the New Living Translation®.

Let's talk about it...

God has no favorites. As Peter and Cornelius discovered, the only thing it takes to join God's people is faith in Jesus. It doesn't matter if you are rich or poor, tall or short, clumsy or athletic, from Australia or down the street, or *anything*. Jesus died for *all* people and wants *all* of us to be a part of God's family.

Yes, God will bless us,
and people all over the world will fear him.
Psalm 67:7, NLT

Peter's Amazing Rescue

God answers prayers in many different ways. You never know what God is going to do. In this story some believers find that God answered their prayers in a completely surprising way.

Discover how God did more than they ever imagined...

King Herod Agrippa began to hurt some believers in the church. When Herod saw how much this pleased the Jewish leaders, he put Peter in jail during the Passover celebration. Herod planned to bring Peter out for public trial after the Passover. But while Peter was in jail, the church prayed for him.

The night before Peter's trial, he was asleep, chained between two soldiers, with others standing guard at the gate. Suddenly, there was a bright light in the cell, and an angel of the Lord stood before Peter. The angel woke him and said, "Quick! Get up!" And the chains fell off Peter's wrists. Then the angel ordered, "Get dressed and follow me."

So Peter followed the angel. But all the time he thought he was just dreaming.

After the angel left Peter, he finally figured out what had happened.

Peter went to the home of Mary, the mother of John Mark, where many were praying. He knocked at the door in the gate, and a servant girl named Rhoda came to open it. When she recognized Peter's voice, she was

so happy that, instead of opening the door, she ran
back inside and told everyone, "Peter is at the door!"

But no one really believed Rhoda.

When they finally went out and opened the door,
they were amazed. Peter motioned for them to quiet
down. Then he told them what had happened and how
the Lord had led him out of jail.

Story based on Acts 12:1-17 as it appears in the New Living Translation®.

Let's talk about it...

No one could believe what God had done. Peter
thought he was just dreaming. And Rhoda was so
surprised to see Peter that she just left him outside! But
once everyone figured out what had happened, they
were very excited. God had answered their prayers.
God always hears our prayers. Watch for the surprising
ways that God answers yours.

I will answer them before they even call to me.
While they are still talking to me about their needs,
I will go ahead and answer their prayers!
Isaiah 65:24, NLT

Whose Side Are You On?

When have you had to choose sides? It can be an important decision. You get lumped with everyone on your side, whether they do good or bad things. In this story Paul and Bar-Jesus had different sides.

Decide who was on the right side...

Sent out by the Holy Spirit, Paul and Barnabas sailed for the island of Cyprus. There, in the town of Salamis, they went to the Jewish synagogues and preached the Word of God. (John Mark went with them as their helper.)

They preached from town to town across the whole island until finally they reached Paphos. There they met a Jewish sorcerer, a false prophet named Bar-Jesus. He stayed close to the governor, Sergius Paulus, who was a very smart man.

The governor invited Barnabas and Paul to visit him, for he wanted to hear the Word of God. But Bar-Jesus stepped in and told the governor to pay no attention to what Paul and Barnabas said. He was trying to turn the governor away from the Christian faith.

Then Paul, filled with the Holy Spirit, looked the sorcerer in the eye and said, "You son of the Devil, full of every sort of trick. You are an enemy of all that is good. Will you never stop trying to get in the way of the Lord? And now the Lord will touch you with punishment, and you will be made blind." Instantly darkness fell upon him, and he began wandering

around begging for someone to take his hand and lead him.

When the governor saw what had happened, he believed what he learned about the Lord.

Story based on Acts 13:4-12 as it appears in the New Living Translation®.

Jailhouse Rock

Sometimes people get mad at us, even when we are trying to do something good. It's hard to know what to do when that happens. Paul and Silas were thrown into prison for helping someone.

Look at how they reacted...

Once there was a demon-possessed slave girl. She earned a lot of money for her masters by telling fortunes. She followed Paul and Silas around shouting, "These men are servants of the Most High God, and they have come to tell you how to be saved."

This went on day after day. Finally Paul got so tired of it that he made the demon leave the girl.

The girl's masters' hopes of wealth were gone, so they grabbed Paul and Silas and dragged them to the city rulers.

A mob formed against Paul and Silas, and the city rulers ordered them beaten and thrown into prison.

Paul and Silas were praying and singing hymns to God in prison. The other prisoners were listening. Suddenly, there was a great earthquake, and the doors flew open, and the chains of every prisoner fell off! The jailer thought the prisoners had escaped, so he drew his sword to kill himself. But Paul shouted, "Don't do it! We are all here!"

Trembling with fear, the jailer called for lights and ran to Paul and Silas. He brought them out and asked, "What must I do to be saved?"

They answered, "Believe on the Lord Jesus and you will be saved, along with everyone in your house." Then Paul and Silas shared the word of the Lord with all who lived in his household. The jailer washed their wounds, and he and everyone in his household were baptized.

Story based on Acts 16:16-33 as it appears in the New Living Translation®.

Let's talk about it...

It would have been easy for Paul and Silas to get angry for the way they were treated. But when they didn't get angry, people noticed that they were different. And it made the jailer want to know about God. As Christians, we need to treat people with love, even when they treat us badly. That kind of love gets everyone's attention.

Don't repay evil for evil. Don't retaliate when people say unkind things about you. Instead, pay them back with a blessing. That is what God wants you to do, and he will bless you for it.

1 Peter 3:9, NLT

A Plot to Kill

It's not always easy to follow Jesus. Kids may tease you because you go to church. Or they may laugh when they see you carry a Bible. Sometimes, Christians are hurt or even killed for what they believe.
Read about what happened to Paul...

A group of more than forty Jews got together. They promised not to eat or drink anything until they had killed Paul. They went to the religious leaders and told them what they had done. Then they said, "You and the high council should talk to the commander. Tell him to bring Paul back because you want to ask him more questions. But we will kill him on the way."

But Paul's nephew heard the plan and told Paul. Paul called one of the officers and said, "Take this young man to the commander. He has something important to tell him."

When the officer did, the commander took Paul's nephew by the arm, led him aside, and asked, "What is it you want to tell me?"

Paul's nephew told him, "Some Jews are going to ask you to bring Paul before the council tomorrow. They are pretending they want to get some more information. But there are more than forty men hiding along the way ready to kill him."

"Don't let anyone know you told me this," the commander warned.

Then the commander called two of his officers and ordered them to get soldiers ready to take Paul safely

to Governor Felix. Then he wrote a letter to the governor
to explain why Paul was being sent to him.

So that night, as ordered, the soldiers took Paul as
far as Antipatris.

Story based on Acts 23:12-31 as it appears in the New Living Translation®.

Let's talk about it...

Paul probably wasn't surprised that people wanted to
kill him. Satan always tries to cause trouble for Christians
whenever God is doing something great. Our lives as
Christians may not always be easy and safe. In fact,
Jesus warns his followers that they *will* face troubles.
But Jesus also promises that he will *always* be with us.

And be sure of this: I am with you always,
even to the end of the age.
Matthew 28:20, NLT

Safe at Last!

Think about a time when your family drove through a terrible storm. Remember what it felt like to finally get home? Safe at last! In this story Paul's journey took him through a wild storm and a shipwreck.
Find out why Paul was not afraid...

Paul and several other prisoners were put in the care of an army officer and placed on a ship. They had several days of rough sailing, but they finally arrived at Fair Havens, near the city of Lasea. The weather was becoming dangerous for long voyages. Paul spoke to the ship's officers about it.

Paul said, "I believe there is trouble ahead if we go on—shipwreck and danger to our lives." But the crew wanted to go farther up the coast. So they sailed along, staying close to shore. But the weather changed suddenly, and a wind of typhoon strength blew the ship out to sea. They couldn't turn the ship around, so they gave up and let it drift.

The terrible storm raged for many days, blotting out the sun and the stars. All hope was gone. No one had eaten for a long time. Finally, Paul called the crew together and said, "Men, you should have listened to me before and not left Fair Havens. But cheer up! Last night an angel of the God whom I serve told me, 'Don't be afraid, Paul. God will give safety to everyone sailing with you.'"

As morning came, Paul took some bread, gave thanks to God in front of everybody, and ate a piece. Then everyone felt better, and they ate.

The crew saw a bay with a beach. But the ship hit a sandbar and was smashed by the force of the waves.

The commanding officer ordered everyone to swim or float on pieces of the ship. So everyone got safely ashore!

Story based on Acts 27:1-44 as it appears in the New Living Translation®.

Let's talk about it...

Those people must have been so glad to get to shore. They probably thought that they would never get home safely again. God's message to Paul must have made them feel much better. God promises to keep us safe, too. No matter what kind of storms are ahead, remember God's promise to you.

God is my strong fortress; he has made my way safe.
2 Samuel 22:33, NLT

Let Me Introduce Myself

Suppose you are going to meet someone for the first time. What would you tell that person about yourself? You probably want the person to think well of you. But Paul was more concerned about something else.

Here is what Paul first told the Romans...

When Paul arrived in Rome, he was allowed to have his own private room, but he was guarded by a soldier.

Three days after Paul's arrival, he called together the local Jewish leaders. He said to them, "Brothers, I was arrested in Jerusalem, even though I had done nothing against our people or the customs of our ancestors. The Romans asked me many questions. Then they wanted to release me, for they found no reason to kill me. But when the Jewish leaders protested, I felt it necessary to get help from Caesar, even though I had no desire to be against my own people. I asked you to come here today so we could meet. I wanted to tell you that I am chained because I believe that the hope of Israel—the Messiah—has already come."

They said, "We have heard nothing against you. But we want to hear what you believe, for all we know about these Christians is that people everywhere are speaking against them."

So a large number of people came to Paul's house. He told them about the Kingdom of God and taught them about Jesus from the Scriptures. Some believed and some didn't. But they left with this final word from Paul:

"I want you to know that God's salvation is also open to the non-Jewish people, and they will accept it."

For the next two years, Paul lived in his own rented house. He welcomed all who visited him.

Story based on Acts 28:16-30 as it appears in the New Living Translation®.

Let's talk about it...

Paul couldn't say anything about himself without mentioning Jesus—that's how important Jesus was to Paul. When we follow Jesus, it should affect everything we are and everything we do. Jesus becomes the most important thing in our lives. And we want to tell others about him.

This letter is from Paul, Jesus Christ's slave,
chosen by God to be an apostle
and sent out to preach his Good News.

Romans 1:1, NLT

Some Good Advice

Sometimes you just don't know what to do. That's when you need good advice. Getting advice from older and wiser people can be a big help. This is a letter from Paul to his younger friend Timothy.

Listen to Paul's advice...

Timothy, I thank God for you, and I remember you in my prayers. I will be very happy when we are together again.

I know that you really trust the Lord, for you have the faith of your mother and your grandmother. God has not given us a spirit of fear, but of power, love, and self-control. So you must never be ashamed to tell others about our Lord. And don't be ashamed of me, either, even though I'm in prison for Christ. With the strength God gives you, be ready to handle trouble with me for Christ.

It is God who saved us and chose us to live a holy life. He did not do this because we deserved it. He always planned to show his love and kindness to us through Christ Jesus. And now he has made all of this plain to us by the coming of Christ Jesus. He broke the power of death and showed us the way to life forever through the Good News.

Share my trouble, as a good soldier of Christ Jesus. And as Christ's soldier, do not let yourself become too busy with the things of everyday life. If you do, you cannot please the one who has put you in his army.

Follow the Lord's rules for doing his work, just as an athlete either follows the rules or is out and wins no prize. Hardworking farmers are the first to enjoy the fruit of their work. Think about what I am saying. The Lord will give you understanding in all these things.

Story based on 2 Timothy 1:3-2:7 as it appears in the New Living Translation®.

Let's talk about it...

What parts of Paul's advice could help you? It's great to get help from the advice in the Bible. But it's also good to have an older person who can help us when we have a question or an important decision to make. Parents, grandparents, older brothers and sisters, and people at church can be great advice-givers. Next time you need advice, just ask!

People who despise advice will find themselves in trouble; those who respect it will succeed.

Proverbs 13:13, NLT

203

A New World

Do you like smelly garbage? Do you like skinning your knees? Do you like it when people are mean? None of us like those nasty things. And one day, when Jesus comes back, everything bad will go away.

See what it will be like...

Then I [John] saw a new heaven and a new earth. The old heaven and the old earth had disappeared. And the sea was also gone. And I saw the new Jerusalem, coming down out of heaven like a beautiful bride.

I heard a loud shout from the throne, saying, "Look, the home of God is now among his people! He will live with them, and they will be his people. And there will be no more death or sorrow or crying or pain. For the old world and its evils are gone forever."

And the one sitting on the throne said, "Look, I am making all things new!" And then he said to me, "Write this down, for what I tell you is trustworthy and true."

So he took me in spirit to a great, high mountain, and he showed me the holy city, Jerusalem. It was filled with the glory of God and sparkled like an expensive jewel, crystal clear like jasper.

No temple could be seen in the city, for the Lord God Almighty and the Lamb are its temple. And the city has no need of sun or moon, for the glory of God shines on the city, and the Lamb is its light. The nations of the earth will walk in its light, and the rulers of the world will come and bring their glory to it. Its gates never close at the end of day because there is no night. And

all the nations will bring their glory and honor into the city. Nothing evil will be allowed to enter—no one who does what is wrong or tells lies—but only those whose names are written in the Lamb's Book of Life.

Story based on Revelation 21:1-27 as it appears in the New Living Translation®.

Let's talk about it...

The new city of Jerusalem sounds wonderful, doesn't it? It will be beautiful and holy. Nothing ugly or evil or hurtful will be there. Everything will be made new. When we are sad because of the bad things that can happen in this world, think about this. Some day soon God's new Kingdom will come and all evil will go away forever!

Look! I am creating new heavens and a new earth—
so wonderful that no one will even think
about the old ones anymore.
Isaiah 65:17, NLT

THE NLT™ STORY BIBLE SERIES

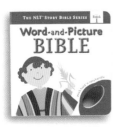

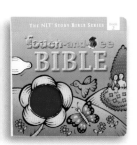

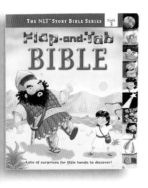

Seven Books, Seven Reasons.

The **NLT**™ Story Bible Series is the easy choice. Here's why:

Reason 1 — It covers every age and stage of your child's development.

It grows with your child from birth to twelve. **Reason 2**

Reason 3 — The **NLT**™ is today's most popular new Bible version.

It's easy for your child to understand because the **NLT**™ is user-friendly. **Reason 4**

Reason 5 — It's easy for you to choose just the right book for your child.

It was developed with input from best-selling author and child development expert Dr. Mary Manz Simon. **Reason 6**

Reason 7 — It's published by Standard Publishing, the leader in children's Bible storybooks.

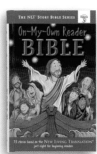

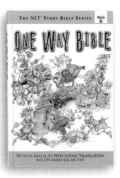

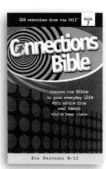

Word-and-Picture Bible
Item no: **04141**
ISBN: **0-7847-1594-7**

Touch-and-See Bible
Item no: **04142**
ISBN: **0-7847-1595-5**

Flap-and-Tab Bible
Item no: **04143**
ISBN: **0-7847-1596-3**

Play-and-Learn Bible
Item no: **04144**
ISBN: **0-7847-1597-1**

On-My-Own Reader Bible
Item no: **04145**
ISBN: **0-7847-1598-X**

One Way Bible
Item no: **04146**
ISBN: **0-7847-1599-8**

Connections Bible
Item no: **04147**
ISBN: **0-7847-1500-9**

Standard
PUBLISHING™

www.standardpub.com